CRASH!

How Things Worked

Robin Einhorn and Richard R. John, Series Editors

CRASH!

*How the Economic Boom & Bust
of the 1920s Worked*

PHILLIP G. PAYNE

Johns Hopkins University Press | *Baltimore*

© 2015 Johns Hopkins University Press
All rights reserved. Published 2015
Printed in the United States of America on acid-free paper

9 8 7 6 5 4 3 2 1

Johns Hopkins University Press
2715 North Charles Street
Baltimore, Maryland 21218-4363
www.press.jhu.edu

Library of Congress Cataloging-in-Publication Data

Payne, Phillip G.
    Crash! : how the economic boom and bust of the 1920s worked / Phillip G. Payne.
        pages cm. — (How things worked)
    Includes bibliographical references and index.
    ISBN 978-1-4214-1855-1 (hardback) — ISBN 1-4214-1855-X (hardback) —
ISBN 978-1-4214-1856-8 (paperback) — ISBN 1-4214-1856-8 (paperback) —
ISBN 978-1-4214-1857-5 (electronic) — ISBN 1-4214-1857-6 (electronic) 1. United States —
Economic conditions — 1918–1945. 2. United States — Economic policy — To 1933.
3. Depressions — 1929 — United States. 4. Stock Market Crash, 1929. I. Title.
    HC106.3.P3517 2015
    330.973'0915 — dc23

                                2015008453

A catalog record for this book is available from the British Library.

Special discounts are available for bulk purchases of this book. For more information,
please contact Special Sales at 410-516-6936 or specialsales@press.jhu.edu.

Johns Hopkins University Press uses environmentally friendly book materials,
including recycled text paper that is composed of at least 30 percent
post-consumer waste, whenever possible.

CONTENTS

PREFACE

During the 2008 fall semester, the stock market collapsed. Putting aside that financial crises tend to happen in the fall, it was simply a coincidence that I was teaching my usual history surveys when reality presented a real, and scary, teaching opportunity. The desperation underscored the importance of learning historical lessons. Panic consumed Wall Street. Journalists and politicians, champions of modern financial companies as "too big to fail," watched in horror as they failed. The housing market that had promised never-ending prosperity led the economy into a downward spiral. The size, technology, and globalized interconnectivity that made the banks seemingly invincible contributed to the spreading financial contagion. The George W. Bush administration and Congress hotly debated bailing out the banks. The Federal Reserve Board intervened in the markets, assuming unprecedented responsibilities. The financial system froze, credit stopped, and the public heard the phrase "moral hazard," a lot. Journalists, politicians, and pundits now spoke of the worst financial crisis since 1929.

As things fell apart, students who often tended to show little interest in finance or economics asked some fundamental and basic questions. What just happened? How do the markets work? What would happen? Was this the beginning of a new Depression? These are the sort of questions that led to this book, which looks at how the boom of the 1920s and the bust of the 1930s, hinging on the stock market crash of 1929, worked. In *Crash!* I use the central question of the series, How Things Worked, to explore the questions that my students asked me in 2008.

In telling a very complex, and politicized, story I returned to some basic questions. How did it work? What was the context? With this in mind I explain how the stock market of the 1920s worked as well as discuss topics that set the stage for the boom and speculative markets. The New Era economy of the 1920s was a classic study of an economic boom fueled by ever rising expectations. Boosters eagerly touted new technologies, new financial practices, and new ways of doing business. In addition to the actual crash, I examine the aftermath as the Depression settled onto the nation. The New Deal changed finance in the United States until the end of the twentieth century.

I am grateful to Robert J. Brugger, senior editor at Johns Hopkins University Press, for his patience and help in figuring out how to tell this story in an accessible way. If I had realized the difficulty of turning this complex story into a readable account, I might not have taken on the challenge. Bob's feedback and guidance proved invaluable. I also have to thank Kathryn Marguy, editorial assistant at the Press, for her patience and diligence. Rachel Rodriguez read an early draft while a student at St. Bonaventure. The librarians at Friedsam Library at St. Bonaventure were, as ever, professional and helpful. My wife, Penny, was supportive, as always. As with so many things, discussing this project with her proved invaluable and insightful. My children, Russell and Laurel, heard more than they wanted to about early twentieth-century economic history. I hope it wasn't too much of a burden.

CRASH!

Prologue: How Panic Spreads

On November 8, 1929, bank president James J. Riordan commit-ted suicide. That Friday he entered the County Trust Company in New York City, removed a gun from a teller's cage, returned home, and shot himself. The next morning his sister found his body upstairs in an overstuffed chair. Aside from being a private tragedy, his death had far-reaching implications. It held the potential to feed the fear that spread after the stock market crash of Octo-ber 1929. The crash terrified investors, which is why they called these crashes "panics." Shortly after the market crashed, stories appeared that ruined stock-brokers, and speculators committed suicide. Riordan's death seemed to be another instance of a ruined banker taking his own life, so Country Trust officials needed to protect the bank from the possibility of people losing faith, panicking, and demanding their money.

To keep customer confidence, the bank brought in John Raskob and Al Smith, two men of enormous stature and influence. A high-profile business-man, Raskob may be best known today for building the Empire State Building. During the twenties, Raskob promoted the stock market and dabbled in poli-tics, helping his friend Al Smith run for president in 1928 on the Democratic ticket. Smith, the former governor of New York, was the first Catholic to be nominated by a major political party for the presidency. He had groomed the current governor, Franklin D. Roosevelt, for office. Bringing in power brokers like Smith and Raskob signaled the seriousness of the situation. If bank customers panicked, all would be lost.

The stories of stockbrokers and speculators paying for their hubris by flinging themselves from buildings onto Wall Street had a great deal of popular appeal. After the crash, investors lost faith in the markets and nouveau riche millionaires became paupers overnight. Banks once considered bastions of sound, innovative business practices failed. The death of Riordan, a bank president, fit that pattern. Indeed, reading press accounts of his death, one could think people were more concerned with the fate of his bank than the tragedy of his death.

Riordan's death became part of the narrative of the crash. Reports soon emerged that Al Smith had convinced the public investigator not to release news of Riordan's death until after the bank closed for business at 1 o'clock on Saturday. Although the press later criticized this withholding of information, city and bank officials went along out of fear of a bank run, when customers mobbed the bank demanding their deposits. A run could easily wipe out the bank. Bank officials quickly brought in auditors to prove the solvency of the bank. Raskob and Smith convened a press conference to reassure a nervous public that the bank president's death had nothing to do with the bank itself. Raskob became the temporary chairman. New York City announced that it was leaving $3 million in deposits with the bank as a gesture of confidence. To make sure the public understood, the US Trucking Corporation pulled up and delivered three trunks of money under heavy guard. Bank leaders went out of their way to let the public know the bank was sound with cash on hand.

The County Trust Company did, indeed, prove solvent but not so Riordan personally. Riordan left $438,295 in assets, but claims against his estate amounted to over $900,000. Smith received over $44,000 in repayment of loans he had made to Riordan. In this sense hubris and the crash did contribute to Riordan's suicide, but his death was an anomaly and not the norm.

One prominent economist and student of the Great Depression investigated the story of suicides following the stock market crash and found them exaggerated. He laid out the suicide rates and took into account various factors. The suicide rate did increase slightly in the years following the crash, but that trend started in the 1920s, before the crash. He wrote, "One can only guess how the suicide myth became established. Like alcoholics and gamblers, broken speculators are supposed to have a propensity for self-destruction. At a time when broken speculators were plentiful, the newspapers and the public may have simply supplied the corollary" (130).[1] With the Riordan suicide, you can see the concern that, with a jittery public, it might trigger a bank run.

Public reaction also played a role in two other celebrity financier suicides, which seemed to contribute to public desire for a comeuppance but also fed the fear that infected the markets. On March 12, 1932, Ivar Kreuger shot himself in his Paris apartment. Local officials withheld the news until the Wall Street markets closed. They defended their actions by reminding critics that Smith had withheld news of Riordan's death three years before. Kreuger, a Swiss businessman and financier, had been famous as the "Match King," for his plan—many said scheme—to make investors wealthy through securing match monopolies. Kreuger had achieved an international reputation for financial wizardry, business acumen, and philanthropy. Following his death, investigators found widespread deception in his financial empire, the failure of which rocked Wall Street, creating the "Kreuger Crash." With the market crashing again and the nation at the depths of the Great Depression, Congress passed legislation regulating Wall Street.

Kreuger's suicide and the subsequent discovery of his swindling came as a shock, the fall of a hero. The public, however, did not consider Jesse Livermore, "the great bear of Wall Street," a hero when he killed himself in 1940. By 1940 the Depression had neared an end, but Livermore retained a status as one of the villains of Wall Street. Livermore specialized in making money from a declining market. He bet that companies would fail. In 1907 and in 1929 he successfully predicted crashes and bet against the market (otherwise known as short selling). He then made a massive fortune, $100 million, short selling in October 1929, but by the mid-1930s he had lost the fortune. In 1940, nearly broke, he lost his trading license. He shot himself, leaving a suicide note for his wife explaining his failures. Livermore understood the mass psychology of the fear that accompanied bursting bubbles, citing as his favorite book Charles Mackay's *Extraordinary Popular Delusions and the Madness of Crowds*.

Mackay's book, written in the middle of the nineteenth century, demonstrates that, although the financial instruments and tools may change, some of the underlying dynamics of bubbles remain the same. Mackay argued that previous financial bubbles resulted from manias, mass popular delusions that someone has discovered easy money. For all the complications of modern finance and economics, the simple underlying fact remains that if a lot of people want to make easy money betting on stocks (or something else), they will ignore facts that warn them otherwise. After the bubble burst, perhaps those same people needed to believe that their enablers, the stockbrokers, boosters, and bankers, would likely kill themselves. As we will see, mass psychology helps to explain how speculation generally and, in particular, the stock market crash of 1929 worked.

For now I leave you with the simple fact that fear drove the markets in October 1929.

1 How in the 1920s the American Economy Promoted Speculation

Richard Whitney: Hero to Villain

On October 24, 1929, Black Thursday, Richard Whitney strode onto the recently renovated trading floor of the New York Stock Exchange. Amid the chaos of one of the worst stock market crashes in history, he bid high for shares in US Steel. As panic fueled a crashing market, with many sellers unable to find buyers, Whitney's bid held the promise of saving the day. Unsold stocks had no one to buy them—air pockets, in the parlance of the traders—so the stocks plunged toward worthlessness. Whitney, paying above-market prices, represented the bankers' attempt to fill the air pockets, boost confidence, and end the panic selling. Whitney's mission was to end the fear. It did not work.

October 1929 is a pivotal moment in history. Typically, historians tell you that the change from one decade to another is arbitrary, but 1929 did mark the end of one era and the beginning of another. Throughout the 1920s it seemed the American stock market had become an unstoppable money-making machine. Politicians, voters, bankers, journalists, and many others bought into the promise of easy riches. The October 1929 market crash ended the boom; fear replaced optimism. The stock market would not recover for a generation, the economy for over a decade. You can see this in Richard Whitney's story. Whitney, part of a celebrated banking family during the boom of the 1920s and hero of the crash, became a public villain by the middle of the Depression decade.

In a speculative market the "greater fool" is the last person holding the stock when the bubble bursts. Yet, there stood Whitney, buying high as literally everyone else sold. It would seem a foolish move. However, on that day Whitney did not act as an investor or the greater fool. Whitney needed to change the psychology of the crowd.

Whitney's importance went beyond buying; he bought for the "organized support." Led by the partners at J. P. Morgan and Company, the elite bankers of Wall Street had assembled to combat the panic. They had seen the dynamics of panics and bank runs before. The bankers followed past practice; they flooded the market with money. Legendary financier J. P. Morgan had performed a similar service in the Panic of 1893 that saved the gold standard and bailed out the administration of President Grover Cleveland. During the Bankers' Panic of 1907, Morgan organized a pool that flooded the street with money boosting prices and saving banks. He organized a bailout after the Treasury Department in Teddy Roosevelt's administration failed. In 1893 and 1907 Morgan and his associates dealt with financial panics better than the government. The same seemed to be the case in 1929, when Whitney had the backing of the leading Wall Street bankers. Their money would prop up the markets and convince the public not to panic. Symbolically, Whitney began his buying spree with US Steel, the crowning accomplishment of the senior J. P. Morgan's career.

Richard Whitney's identity, his social standing, spoke to the need to reassure investors. Whitney represented the clubby, old boys' network that made up Wall Street. Those who followed Wall Street, a popular pastime in the 1920s, recognized Whitney as the New York Stock Exchange's vice president and, perhaps more importantly, the brother of George Whitney, a partner at J. P. Morgan and Company and the presumed successor to bank president Thomas Lamont. J. P. Morgan Jr. could not organize the pool, as his father had done, because he was traveling in Europe, so Lamont organized the bankers. People in the know recognized that Whitney represented Wall Street's elite.

In the long term, however, we know that Whitney's efforts failed. The bankers did not stem the panic. The markets gyrated wildly, but ultimately the crash of 1929 went down as one of the great financial disasters. Following the crash, the New York Stock Exchange promoted Whitney to president, confirming his status as the consummate insider and hero of the day. During the 1930s Whitney, like many bankers, testified before an angry Congress and defended the integrity of Wall Street's practices against New Deal regulations with aristocratic aplomb. Whitney fell from grace when his finances fell apart in scandal. The defender of high finance had embezzled from the New York Yacht Club and the Stock Exchange gratuity fund. He used his wife's and brother's fortunes to cover it up. Richard owed his brother George a lot of money. Whitney went from hero of the 1920s to villain of the 1930s, finishing the decade in Sing Sing prison.

How did we get to the moment when Whitney needed to attempt heroics to stop the panic? The 1929 crash remains a complicated and controversial topic. For the moment, let us set aside the theories and controversies to walk through the 1920s economy to place the Great Bull Market and its crash in context.

Greater Fools

When we think of the 1920s, images of the Jazz Age spring to mind; scenes from the *Great Gatsby* of opulent wealth, speakeasies, flappers, and lavish parties funded by the Great Bull Market. Conservatives like Warren Harding, Calvin Coolidge, and Herbert Hoover served in the White House, preaching the virtues of small government and big business. Journalists dubbed the boom the Coolidge Prosperity, when business ruled. However, at some point the Bull Market became the speculative bubble that burst in 1929. All markets have speculation, but sometime around 1927 or 1928 speculation started dominating the stock market. The reason for the ambiguity is that there is not a clear-cut definition of how to separate speculation from investing (or gambling). For the sake of simplicity, speculation is a form of gambling, of taking a financial risk, which became a popular pastime in the twenties. All markets have some gambling or risk taking (indeed, this can be a good thing), so there is not a moment in time when the market crossed the line into speculative mania. Journalists, policy makers, and scholars more often than not recognize a speculative bubble after the fact, in the wreckage of the collapse. The late 1920s market had many features commonly associated with a speculative bubble fueled by the mania of the crowds.

To add to our definition, speculation might be that people buy something for the purpose of resale without interest in inherent value or producing a commodity. Speculators look to flip the thing. The 1920s saw real economic growth built on innovation and new technologies, but the stock market became disconnected from that. People bought and sold stocks with little or no concern for the health or value of the company issuing the stock. During a bubble people convince themselves that a commodity's value—stocks in the 1920s—will go up forever. There is a mania for buying. You can't lose. It is a sure bet.

Boosters promote the idea that a new development, often a technology, has changed the rules of the game. The twenties saw what later generations would refer to as a "tech bubble." Radio in the twenties, similar to the Internet in the nineties, had boosters who heralded the power of the technology to permanently transform the economy with never-ending prosperity. Boosters called it the New Era economy. During the 1990s the Internet created the New Economy and the dot.com bubble. During the housing bubble of the early twenty-first century, boosters argued that changes to the mortgage industry meant that house prices would go up forever. Regardless of the commodity or the technology, the idea is the same. The rules have changed. Only a fool would not get in on it. This fuels the buying mania. Why not buy high? It will only go higher. However, bubbles end. Once the panic starts, prices fall because there are no buyers. Whatever you do, do not be the fool caught holding the bag when the bubble bursts.

In retrospect, it is easy to say, "Of course the stock market bubble crashed," but for those living in the 1920s questioning the peace and prosperity, a New Era of technological and business innovation, did not seem obvious. Intellectuals of the 1920s worried that consumerism and crass materialism would undermine the American character, not that the party would end but that it would never end. The twenties' prosperity started as America recovered from World War I and saw the development of new technologies and businesses, but by the late 1920s stocks had assumed the role of the new thing, the game changer that kept making money. This brings us back to Whitney's buying spree in October 1929. Whitney, in this scenario, boosted the bubble by trying to convince people to continue buying, to restore the investors' confidence. Who did Whitney need to reenter the market? He needed the general public to regain confidence, not just to leave their money in the bank, but also to continue investing in Wall Street. The 1920s saw, for the first time in American history, average people in large numbers investing in stocks and following the market.

The crash was important, not only because people had invested money in the market, but the nation had invested emotionally in it as well. Not all the investors had Richard Whitney's pedigree or family connections with which to paper over losses. Legend has it that brokers and bankers, ruined by the crash, leapt from buildings. Bodies, however, did not rain on Wall Street. Whitney's story of corruption proved more typical than Riordan's suicide. Investigations found a rise in embezzling during the boom. The crash ruined honest bankers and traders but did not bring the tragedy of brokers flinging themselves from ledges. Instead, the tragedy consisted of the average man or woman who bought into the bubble only to be financially ruined. Some of these people did commit suicide.

What Made the New Era Possible?

Bubbles are characterized by a "this time is different" attitude that has at its core an almost willful disregard for history while there is money to be made. Those boosting the bubble have to explain why it isn't like the last time. What made the boosterism plausible? As we saw with Whitney, the public celebrated bankers and businessmen, some of whom achieved celebrity status. During the 1920s few listened to critics of finance and Wall Street. Historically, in the United States there existed a tradition of criticism of financial capitalism. The populist tradition dating back to Thomas Jefferson and Andrew Jackson had recently manifested in the 1890s populist movement, which attacked the eastern banking establishment. During the 1920s agrarian populism was, by and large, marginalized. During the Progressive Era of the early twentieth century, reformers sought to tame the "money trust" as a form of concentrated power that threatened democracy. Progressive reformers put into place laws and institutions, such as the Federal Reserve Board, that shaped the economy of the twenties.

Progressive reformers sought to regulate and bust up what they called the "money trust," the bankers and businessmen who had dominated the Gilded Age. Progressives echoed the older critique when they spoke of restoring democracy, of a fight between "the people and the interest." By "the interest," they meant the power of concentrated wealth found in the big businesses that rose during the Gilded Age. Muckraking journalists exposed the corrupt power of the trusts exemplified by J. P. Morgan. The two progressive presi-

First Mate J. P. Morgan helps Captain John D. Rockefeller steer the ship of finance. Morgan and Rockefeller working together personified what critics referred to as the "money trust," the idea that banks and big businessmen formed a cartel that undermined democracy. *Source:* Bob Satterfield, via Wikimedia Commons (public domain).

dents, Theodore Roosevelt and Woodrow Wilson, acted to reign in the money trust and its impact on the economy and finance.

As the first Progressive Era president, Roosevelt railed against the "malefactors of great wealth." Roosevelt's ascension to the presidency upon the death of the business-friendly William McKinley in 1901 shocked business leaders. Roosevelt viewed Wall Street bankers as an undeserving wealthy aristocracy, a threat to American rugged individualism and democracy. Roosevelt's trust-busting brought him into direct conflict with J. P. Morgan, the great builder of consolidated business (aka the trusts that Roosevelt wanted to bust). However, during the Bankers' Panic of 1907 Roosevelt and Morgan worked together out of necessity.

The 1907 panic forced Roosevelt and Morgan into an unlikely alliance, setting in motion legislation that shaped the 1920s. The Panic of 1907, like most financial panics, has a complicated backstory. For our purposes it is enough to know that the fallout of an unsuccessful attempt to corner the market on shares of the United Copper Company resulted in widespread bank failures. Credit tightened, and the money supply contracted. The US Treasury Department stepped in, but it lacked the resources and the tools to deal with the panic. The treasury ran out of money. Then the bankers turned to J. P. Morgan to organize a pool to save the market, which is one of the reasons bankers looked to his bank and his son, J. P. Morgan Jr., in 1929.

The Panic of 1907 served as a lesson in 1929 for bankers and government officials. Both panics resulted in bank runs during which people lined up to withdraw their money, fearing that it would be lost if the bank went under. Of course, banks did not keep the entirety of their assets as cash in the building. However, if a bank or trust reached a point where it could not give money to depositors it would be ruined. In the event of a run, bankers looked to slow the process without shutting their doors—for example, ordering their tellers to work slowly. Most importantly, they needed to find cash from wealthy investors or, more likely, other banks. Shared board members and common investments connected banks, so the failure of a large bank could threaten other banks. If big enough, it could threaten the financial system. If a run spread into the broader financial section, a pool might form a large pot of money that would be used strategically for deposits, loans, or stock purchases. This is what happened in 1907 and is why Richard Whitney walked onto the trading floor in 1929.

After the Panic of 1907 bankers and government officials looked to find a way to prevent, or at least contain, future crashes. The movement led to the creation of the Federal Reserve Board. Financial leaders and policy makers wanted to take steps to prevent panics but also to systemize the response. In Europe national banks acted to stabilize the financial system. However, the United States had not had a national bank since Andrew Jackson destroyed the Second Bank of the United States. In 1907 J. P. Morgan acted as the de facto national bank. Although Morgan had saved the financial sector, people worried that he and his fellow bankers had too much power. Following the panic, Congress held hearings resulting in competing plans to create a national bank and deal with future financial crises.

Wall Street bankers, particularly the partners at J. P. Morgan, supported creating a national bank on the model of the Bank of England. This idea was an old one. The first secretary of the treasury, Alexander Hamilton, based the First Bank of the United States on the Bank of England. Bankers hoped it would formalize the pools and create a more flexible currency. Paul Warburg, a Jewish German immigrant, led the Wall Street bankers advocating for a central bank and is often referred to as the father of the Federal Reserve. In 1910 Republican senator Nelson Aldrich, known for his close ties to banking and J. P. Morgan in particular, hosted a "duck hunt" on Jekyll Island, at which prominent politicians and bankers hammered out a proposal for a national bank. The Aldrich Plan called for the establishment of a reserve system composed of private bankers and a private central bank that would serve as a lender of last resort during a panic, as the financial agent of the US government, and have regional offices. Under this plan, the central bank would not be part of the national government.

Partisan politics became a factor as the House of Representatives, controlled by the Democratic Party, convened the Pujo Committee, a subcommittee of the House Committee on Banking and Currency, to investigate the "money trust." In investigating the money trust, for the first time the committee successfully gained access to banking records. It also called bankers, including Morgan, to testify. The committee issued a plan to change the nation's banking, including increased oversight and regulations to encourage competition.

Progressive attorney Louis Brandeis used the committee's findings to write *Other People's Money—and How the Bankers Use It*, which first appeared as a series of articles and then as a book. Brandeis argued that a money trust existed and that it stifled competition. Brandeis, a committed foe of concentrated power, argued that when bankers colluded to prevent competition and when they took risks in the markets with their customers' money they violated a trust. Furthermore, bankers colluded with big businesses to form the money trust, an intricate web of connected boards of directors who conspired to suppress competition. As Brandeis saw it, the resulting inefficiency led to higher cost for the consuming public. Therefore, banks needed public oversight and regulations to increase competition.

"I Like a Little Competition" - J. P. Morgan

J. P. Morgan famously testified before the Pujo Committee, which investigated the role of the money trust in the Panic of 1907. Morgan offered a defense of Wall Street and the financial sector. Not all Americans shared his view. The committee's findings became the basis for Brandeis's *Other People's Money* and a stepping stone in the creation of the Federal Reserve Board. Some politicians worried that monopolies were destroying competition. When asked if he disliked competition, his reply inspired this well-known cartoon. *Source:* Art Young, via Wikimedia Commons (public domain).

Going into the 1912 election, the Senate Republicans and the House Democrats had put forward competing plans. The Pujo Committee's recommendations to lessen the power of bankers conflicted with the Aldrich Plan's recommendation to create a powerful private national bank. In an unusual election the three presidential candidates continued the debate, staking out sophisticated positions on the issue of banking. When former president Teddy Roosevelt unsuccessfully challenged incumbent Republican William Howard Taft for the nomination, Roosevelt bolted from the GOP to run as the nominee of the Progressive Party, more commonly known as the Bull Moose Party. The Democrats nominated Woodrow Wilson, a former college professor who had been elected governor of New Jersey, where he had championed progressive causes. Taft ran on the Republican ticket with a traditionally conservative, probusiness platform.

The three candidates vigorously debated how best to deal with the rise of large businesses, particularly banking. Wilson's New Freedom largely followed Brandeis's thinking. Wilson wanted a return to Jeffersonian principles, foreseeing a federal government that injected competition into markets. Roosevelt, on the other hand, advocated a New Nationalism. Roosevelt believed the new, large corporations brought improved efficiencies and other advantages but that the national government needed to ensure that these corporations acted as responsible citizens. He advocated a modern, large government that regulated corporations to protect the common good. The national government would function as an honest broker protecting the needs of the people.

The Democrats won the election of 1912, taking the Senate and the White House, passing economic legislation that had a deep impact on the 1920s. The Pujo Committee's recommendations became the basis for the Clayton Antitrust Act, the Federal Reserve Act, and the Sixteenth Amendment. The Clayton Antitrust Act strengthened the government's ability to break up trusts. The Sixteenth Amendment authorized the income tax, aimed at taxing large fortunes. The Federal Reserve Act, sponsored by Congressman (later, senator) Carter Glass and Senator Robert Latham Owen, created the public Federal Reserve Board, which would oversee the system of affiliated private banks. The Federal Reserve in effect replaced J. P. Morgan, who died in 1913.

The Federal Reserve Act of 1913 created a central bank for the United States and is one of the most important pieces of economic legislation in US history, having a direct impact on the Bull Market of the 1920s and the 1929 crash. Congress created the Federal Reserve System specifically to deal with financial bubbles and panics, but ironically its existence reinforced the "this time is different" attitude of the 1920s New Era. Scholars continue to debate the Federal Reserve's policies during the late 1920s. Did the Federal Reserve contribute to the crash and the Depression?

The Federal Reserve System represented a political compromise between the two plans, blending public and private spheres. The Federal Reserve acts as a bank for banks, as nationally chartered private banks joined a regional Federal Reserve Board. The regional boards, in turn, report to the Federal Reserve Board. Congress and the president designed the Federal Reserve Board to be an independent agency beyond political sway, but board members would be appointed by the president and approved by the Senate. The regional boards had equal power, at least on paper. However, because of its proximity to Wall Street the New York Federal Reserve Bank became the first among equals. Benjamin Strong, as director of the New York Federal Reserve Bank, dominated the Federal Reserve Board in its early years.

The Federal Reserve Board had several new and untested powers, which included raising and lowering interest rates for the money it lent to banks, injecting and removing money from the economy by the buying or selling of treasury bonds, and regulating member banks. A central mission of the Federal Reserve Board would be preventing, or at least ameliorating, panics like that of 1907, by acting as a lender of last resort in the advent of a crash. Among the controversies of creating a national bank, being the lender of last resort ranked high. Critics maintained that the Federal Reserve, by acting as a lender of last resort, made the US government, and hence the taxpayers, liable for losses of private speculators. There would be no penalty for making unwise decisions, thus having the unintended consequence of encouraging recklessness and bubbles. The greater fool would be the Federal Reserve pumping money into a crashing bubble.

Further complicating the situation, politicians had a mixed record in appointing members to the board. While presidents appointed competent bankers such as Benjamin Strong and Paul Warburg, they also appointed cronies with little background in banking or economics. The Federal Reserve opened shop during a critical period of rapid changes to the economy that some of its leaders could not cope with. During its early years the Federal Reserve saw the gold standard unravel and the financial world shift as a result of World War I.

The Nature of Money

One cannot understand the 1920s economy without understanding the changes not just to banking but also to the nature of money. From around

1870 to World War I the United States and European nations subscribed to the gold standard, the idea that a currency is backed by gold. The US government pegged the dollar to gold. Other countries did the same. Nations stored gold in vaults to back their currency. The British played the key role in maintaining the gold standard, but they were hardly alone in supporting it. Bankers held the gold standard as orthodoxy.

Under the gold standard, people could redeem a currency for gold at a fixed rate; therefore, the amount of gold determined the amount of currency in an economy. Increasing the money supply required an increase in the amount of gold through discovery of a new source or trade imbalance. Governments wishing to change the money supply could also change the ratio of gold to currency (i.e., inflating or debasing the currency), but bankers and their political allies considered debasing to be unwise, at best, and more likely the road to economic disaster.

Advocates of the gold standard argued that it had several advantages. The gold standard facilitated international trade by fixing an exchange rate. Using gold as a common benchmark fixed the relative value of different currencies, making it difficult for politicians to manipulate currencies to game international trade or curry favor. A person doing an international transaction would know what an American dollar would be worth in British pounds and that was that. The gold standard acted as an international barometer of trade. A fixed supply of money meant that if an economy grew particularly fast its currency would not inflate, meaning that prices would fall. As prices fell, the cost of that country's exports would also fall and the country would run a trade surplus. The trade surplus meant that gold flowed into the nation, increasing its money supply. This would ultimately restore trade balance.

Central banks acted as the referee in this system. Bankers understood that they would facilitate the flow of gold to restore trade balances. So if a country ran a trade surplus, it would raise interest rates to facilitate the inflow of gold. If a country ran a trade deficit, the central bank would lower interest rates to speed the outflow of gold. Because the gold standard fixed the values of currency, both domestically and relative to other currencies, the standard created a great deal of economic stability with little inflation.

The gold standard had its problems. At times, adherence to the gold standard might run contrary to national policy. Raising interest rates to protect the gold standard could increase unemployment during an economic downturn. The gold standard made it difficult for a central bank to expand a nation's money supply in the event of an emergency, such as a war. Not all countries willingly and consistently followed the rules. New discoveries of gold (i.e., a gold rush) could shock economies.

We can see these potential pitfalls in Europe in the years leading up to World War I. Much has been made of the arms race preceding the war, but central bankers also competed to stockpile gold reserves. Bankers feared, and rightly so, that they would need large supplies of gold to finance a war. Even so, central bankers dramatically underestimated the cost of the war and the amount of gold they would need, setting the stage for the collapse of the gold standard and the rise of American finance on the global stage.

Congress created the Federal Reserve during the waning days of the gold standard. The gold standard, or rather the collapse of the gold standard during World War I, changed the supply of money that helps explain the boom of the 1920s. European nations abandoned the gold standard and borrowed and bought from the United States. By the end of the war the United States was awash in cheap money, a key ingredient for a speculative boom.

The Legacy of the Great War

Herbert Hoover wrote in his memoir, "In a large sense the primary cause of the Great Depression was the war of 1914–1918."[1] Not everyone agreed with Hoover's assessment. While it is not entirely inaccurate, it is also the argument of a former president explaining away the defining disaster of his administration. There is a "don't blame me" element to his statement. One could just as easily argue that World War I set the stage for the American prosperity of the twenties. We can go beyond Hoover's statement to argue that the Great War, in which millions died, nations disappeared, and the political landscape of Europe changed dramatically, is one of the turning points in the history of the world, including the global economy.

The war shifted the center of global financial power from London to New York, transforming the United States from a debtor nation to a creditor nation. To further complicate things, the European powers vastly inflated their currencies, forcing them off the gold standard. Europeans used much of this money to buy American goods, shifting the trade balance in favor of the United States, which found itself with a large trade surplus, European debtors, and a stockpile of gold. With the gold standard broken, there existed no mechanism to force the system back to its previous balance.

When the war broke out, most Americans wanted to heed George Washington's advice to avoid entangling alliances and European troubles. President Wilson pledged that the United States would be neutral in thought and deed. In 1916, Wilson successfully ran for reelection as a peace candidate with the campaign slogans of "He kept Us Out of War" and "Too Proud to Fight." In January 1917 Wilson offered the offices of the United States as a neutral third party to bring "peace without victory" while confirming the United States' long-standing commitment to freedom of the seas and trade among neutral nations. However, German U-Boat attacks and the Zimmerman Telegram led Wilson to ask Congress for a declaration of war. Once the United States entered the war, Wilson attempted to define the terms of the peace with his Fourteen Points, which emphasized self-determination, free trade, and the international diplomatic body of the League of Nations.

Domestically, economic mobilization for the war brought an unusual level of regimentation to the economy. The government drafted nearly 5 million men, removing them from the workforce. The government created a slew of agencies to oversee mobilization. The Division of Planning and Statistics introduced Americans to the idea of a government agency producing economic data, which could be used for planning. The Committee on Public Information (CPI), under the direction of George Creel, sold the war to the public. CPI propaganda advanced the fields of public relations and advertising. When the railroads proved to be an unorganized mess, the Wilson administration nationalized them. Ironically Wilson, who championed the Jeffersonian political tradition, oversaw an expansion of government into the economy that encouraged centralized governmental controls and consolidation of businesses.

The Wilson administration staffed the wartime agencies with "dollar a year men," businessmen who accepted a government salary of $1 to oversee the industries from which they came. Many of these men landed on the War Industries Board (WIB), the agency that planned and managed the purchasing of materials. Financier Bernard Baruch became the WIB's best-known director. Many industrialists, including Henry Ford, disliked him. Partly they disliked an intrusive government agency, but anti-Semitism also played a role. The National War Labor Board and the War Labor Policies Board oversaw labor contracts and disputes. The government seized German chemical patents and ships, turning them over to American companies along with large contracts that jumpstarted the domestic chemical industry. Herbert Hoover headed the Food Administration, which used volunteerism and regulation to organize food production and consumption. The War Finance Corporation oversaw

An appeal that every Victor Dealer will want to answer

The Great War temporarily ended the debate over the role of finance and the money trust. During the war, government war bond drives linked patriotism, investing, and corporate America, setting the stage for the 1920s. The Victor Talking Machine Company encouraged patriotic investing in bonds in October 1918. Worries about the money trust faded as investing and consuming became acts of patriotism. *Source:* Rodgers and Hammerstein Archive of Recorded Sound, The New York Public Library for the Performing Arts, Astor, Lenox and Tilden Foundations (public domain).

funding the war, including Liberty Bond drives. For the first time, during the war the government introduced the masses to the idea not only that the common person should invest but that investing equaled patriotism. Many would carry their investing habits into the new decade.

When the war ended, Wilson led the American delegation to Paris to ne-gotiate the Treaty of Versailles. At this juncture, most histories focus on the fate of the League of Nations. However, for our purposes, the central issues are reparations and debt. This goes to the heart of Hoover's observation that the origins of the Depression can be found in the Great War. The British and the French governments wanted the German government to pay large reparations to punish the Germans and to ease the financial burden of debt repayment and reconstruction. A central debate in European diplomacy for the next decade would be the fairness of German reparations.

As the largest creditor to the European nations, the United States had a stake in the debates over reparations and debt. In 1914 Americans owed for-eigners $3.7 billion. When the war ended in 1919, the United States was owed $12.56 billion, a transformation that concerned both the State Department and Wall Street. Prior to the war J. P. Morgan and Company made its reputa-tion by serving as a representative of London finance in the United States, but now the London branch of J. P. Morgan served the interest of the New York office. Europeans hoped that the Americans would forgive the war debt and grew resentful when they did not. The Germans, however, grew more resentful over the reparations demanded of them. French and British leaders wanted to link Germany's payment of reparations with their ability to repay war loans; US leaders resisted the linkage.

The contentious issues of war debt and reparations complicated the work-ings of the international gold standard. The United States found itself with an extraordinarily large supply of gold. The American stockpile of gold pre-sented a problem for European leaders, particularly the British, who wanted a return to the gold standard as quickly as possible but lacked an adequate reserve. Policy makers continued to hope that gold supply would balance it-self and gold would return to Europe, but this did not happen because of the war-inflated currencies and imbalance of gold. Chancellor of the Exchequer Winston Churchill in 1924 returned Great Britain to the gold standard at prewar exchange rates, with the result being economic disaster. Attempts to force a return to the gold standard would later be cited as one of the causes of the Great Depression.

To summarize, World War I introduced Americans to the idea of buying bonds via Wall Street, associating investing, Wall Street, and patriotism. The war also stimulated industries such as chemical manufacturing and radio. Wartime propaganda paved the way for more sophisticated advertising, and wartime agencies introduced Americans to economic statistics and new forms of organization. The war also left the US banks at the center of the financial world. It would, however, take a few years before these factors manifested in economic growth.

The 1920s Start: The Postwar Recession

Ironically, given the level of planning and organization that went into the war, when it ended the government had no plan for economic demobilization. While campaigning for the Treaty of Versailles, President Wilson suffered incapacitating strokes and disappeared from the public view, creating a leadership vacuum. The government cancelled $2.5 billion in war contracts. With a quarter of the workforce making war goods, many workers found themselves unemployed. Add to that the 2 million servicemen discharged by the military who returned home expecting to find jobs. The economy rapidly deregulated. Following the war strikes swept the nation, 1919 saw more strikes than in any other year in US history, as wartime inflation had eroded workers' purchasing power.

The economy rebounded in the spring of 1919 and continued to grow through the fall on strong spending from pent-up wartime demand. However, by the spring of 1920 this demand ran out. Wholesale prices entered into a severe deflationary recession. Manufacturers cut production. As financial columnist Alexander Noyes has explained, "What happened was simply that demand for goods by the larger consuming public suddenly stopped at the moment when the extraordinarily high prices had stimulated supply."[2] It can be argued that the deflation served as a necessary counter to the wartime inflation, but that does not make it less painful. The recession of 1920–22 saw the gross national product fall by 6 percent, the stock market lost 25 percent, unemployment increased dramatically, 500,000 farmers lost their farms, and 100,000 businesses went bankrupt. Large corporations took huge losses. The Wilson administration offered no effective response. To combat the deflation, the Federal Reserve raised interest rates.

Arguably, farmers felt the pain of the postwar conversion more than most. During the war, agriculture had expanded rapidly while European farm production decreased, eliminating competition. At the same time, demand increased. To meet wartime need, and based on high wartime prices, farmers invested borrowed money in new equipment and land. The tractor, other mechanized farm instruments, and new hybrid seeds increased productivity but also expanded farmers' exposure to the marketplace. When the war came to an end, the bottom fell out of the market just as European farm goods returned to international markets. Farmers had flooded the market and faced a painful contraction.

While many benefited from the cheap food, farmers found it a losing proposition. Why then, as the rest of the economy took off, did agriculture remain in a slump? Farmers confronted the difficulty of an inelastic food market. Farmers could not increase the demand for food. The more farmers grew, the lower prices fell. The lower prices fell, the more farmers had to grow. Demand for new food did not keep pace with the overall prosperity of the decade. In good times people might opt to eat better foods, but people can only eat so much additional food.

Given the generally poor state of the economy, few would have predicted the decade would become known as the Coolidge Prosperity. Instead, Americans feared political upheaval. In the wake of World War I and the Russian Revolution of 1917, Americans feared a conflict between labor and capital; the first Red Scare began. The fears seemed to be realized when, on September 16, 1920, a different type of panic hit Wall Street; no financial bubble burst, nor did customers run on a bank. Rather, a horse-drawn wagon exploded on the corner of Wall and Broad Streets across from 23 Wall Street, home of J. P. Morgan and Company. Amid the chaos thirty-eight people died.[3] The bomber, probably an Italian anarchist, was aiming at the financial power of Wall Street. Despite the violence and unrest, the revolutionary threat that some Americans feared never materialized; instead producers, farmers, and labor unions found themselves out of favor politically.

The bombing, ironically, pointed to Wall Street and a future in which Americans celebrated bankers and not proletariat revolutionaries. When the bomber attacked Wall Street, he acknowledged that World War I had made American bankers the leaders of international finance. That a horse cart delivered the bomb seemed symbolic of the unfolding economic transformation, from the chaos of war to the boom of the 1920s, from the antiquated to the modern. Eventually, the glittering promise of the stock market and not the threat of global anarchism captured the public's imagination.

Babbittry and Bloviating

The president of the United States proved the most ardent New Era booster. In November 1920 Americans elected Warren G. Harding, an Ohio senator and small-town newspaper publisher, who promised a "return to normalcy" during the campaign. The robust and down-to-earth Harding stood in contrast to the cerebral and disabled Wilson. Bitter over the Senate's rejection of the Treaty of Versailles, Wilson wanted to turn the election into a "solemn referendum" on the treaty and the League of Nations. Although physically disabled, Wilson contemplated running for a third term, leaving the Democratic Party in disarray. Wilson's third-term machinations proved unrealistic. Instead, the bitterly divided Democrats nominated James M. Cox, governor of Ohio, for the presidency, and Franklin D. Roosevelt for the vice presidency. Cox's best attributes as a candidate consisted of his moderation, his residency in the important swing state of Ohio, and his lack of connections with Wilson.

The Republicans who met in Chicago, like the Democrats, divided into factions, but for different reasons. Many assumed that the party would nominate Teddy Roosevelt, but he unexpectedly died in 1919. With Roosevelt dead, candidates scrambled to win the nomination, but none emerged as a clear winner. When the convention deadlocked, party leaders turned to Senator Harding.

Harding's campaign foreshadowed the economy of the 1920s, using modern advertising techniques to sell the public a nostalgic vision of simpler times. Republicans signaled an end to Roosevelt-style progressivism by labeling Harding the new McKinley. Harding successfully published a newspaper in his hometown of Marion, Ohio, with the motto of "Boost, Don't Knock." From his newspaper background Harding had entered state politics, rising to the US Senate in 1914. As a presidential nominee, Harding ran a front porch campaign, as had McKinley, that visually reinforced his message of a "return to normalcy." The Harding campaign projected an image of a civic booster surrounded by an idyllic small town, in contrast to the chaos and hardship of the war. By "normalcy," Harding meant a return to "constitutional" government, limited in scope and respecting the checks and balances between the branches. Another Harding campaign slogan, "America First," heralded the emerging isolationism.

In Harding we once again see the combination of the modern with tradition that characterized the decade. Harding evoked an old-fashioned government even as he promised to modernize it with business principles. Harding looked "like a president," something his campaign took advantage of in its advertising. Harding, however, did not reject modernity. Part of the new economy would be consumerism driven by new technologies and the emergence of a much more sophisticated advertising industry. Advertising now created demand rather than simply informing customers. The campaign hired Albert Lasker's advertising firm to help craft the candidate's image. To pique interest, the campaign brought in movie stars. Al Jolson and Mary Pickford both appeared on Harding's front porch. The Chicago Cubs, of whom Lasker owned a minority share, played an exhibition game in Marion for the campaign. Finally, news of Harding's victory arrived over the radio. One could see Hollywood's coming of age and radio as the hot new technology.

Harding brought a civic booster's sensibilities to the White House and, as such, the administration pursued decidedly probusiness policies. The Harding administration cut taxes, eliminated wartime regulations, created the Bureau of the Budget, and cut government spending. Republicans replaced business regulation and trust-busting with a belief in limited government, free markets, and laissez-faire policies. As much as he had done in Marion, Harding saw his job as boosting and harmonizing.

Harding campaigned on the idea of bringing the "best minds" into his administration, by which he meant that he wanted more businessmen in government. He appointed Andrew Mellon secretary of the treasury and Herbert Hoover secretary of commerce. Mellon's qualifications for treasury secretary consisted of being one of the richest men in the country with a background in banking. As a banker he had diversified into a number of other businesses before entering government. Mellon advocated what became known as "trickle down" economics, another thing that lost popularity during the thirties. Entering office Mellon faced a large debt and high, wartime taxes. He theorized that if the government made taxes too high people would avoid paying them. Therefore, Mellon argued, lowering taxes would increase collection and government revenues. With the Revenue Acts of 1921, 1924, and 1926, Congress enacted Mellon's tax cuts.

Herbert Hoover is the other well-known member of Harding's cabinet. Prior to entering politics Hoover made a fortune working in mining engineering and international business. Working in Europe when the war broke out, he began organizing the evacuation of Americans. He then worked with the Commission for Relief in Belgium to provide food for refugees. When the United States entered the war, he joined the Wilson administration as the food administrator to oversee the mobilization of American agriculture. Following the war he again worked in refugee relief, this time with the American Relief Administration. He considered running for president in 1920, but he lacked concrete political affiliations. He had supported Teddy Roosevelt's Progressive Party and worked in a Democratic administration, so many Republicans did not trust his party loyalty.

Harding sought out a position for Hoover in his cabinet, appointing him secretary of commerce. Hoover transformed the Commerce Department from a minor cabinet position into a modern, active agency. He viewed the role of the government as facilitating business efficiency, modernization, and trade. He worked to improve the emerging radio industry and to promote public roads and transportation, and waterworks in the west.

In August 1923 President Harding died in San Francisco. He fell ill on a cross-country "Voyage of Understanding." The presidential party rushed him to the Palace Hotel, where after several days he died. Although today Harding is remembered mostly for scandals that broke after his death, he died a popular president. His popularity stemmed from his genial nature and the economic recovery that began on his watch. His successor, Vice President Calvin Coolidge, would reap the rewards of the rebounding economy.

Calvin Coolidge, the former governor of Massachusetts, did not believe in activist government, preferring to let problems solve themselves. Unusual for a politician, he did not say much (his nickname was Silent Cal), and he did not crave the company of people. As governor he had gained national fame for firing striking Boston police officers. At the 1920 Republican convention, the delegates nominated him for vice president by acclaim. If anything, Coolidge more ardently believed in limited government than Harding. Whereas Harding had liked Hoover, Coolidge considered Hoover a busybody in search of a crisis to solve. Coolidge retained Harding's policies and cabinet, including Hoover and Mellon.[4]

The Republicans' policies of the 1920s had several mainstays. They did not bust trusts. They believed in limited government. While Coolidge favored Mellon's low taxes, he also favored protective tariffs. Under Coolidge, tariffs reached new highs. In the name of government austerity, Coolidge vetoed a veterans' bonus bill, as did Harding, but Congress overrode Coolidge's veto. Coolidge resisted farmers' call for governmental aid, urging farmers to voluntarily reduce production. The powerful farm block crafted the McNary-Haugen Bill to create a federal agency that would purchase surplus agricultural goods to increase domestic prices. The bill failed twice in the Senate, and when it eventually passed Coolidge vetoed it.

Regarding European war debt and German reparations, a central foreign policy of his presidency, Coolidge took the position that the Allies had borrowed the money and had to repay it. Despite the best efforts of British and French diplomats to link German reparations to payment of Allied debt, the United States took the position that no connection existed between the Allies' ability to pay debts and Germany's ability to pay reparations. The European debt crisis became critical, as bankers and diplomats feared that some countries would devalue their currencies. Germany had gone through a period of hyperinflation that led it to replace its currency. When France occupied the Ruhr Valley in an attempt to force Germany to pay, the Coolidge administration decided the time had come to act.

The United States reluctantly became involved in putting together the Dawes Plan. An international body with representatives from the United States, Great Britain, France, Belgium, and Italy met to settle the reparations issue. Indicative of the Coolidge administration, a career diplomat did not lead the American delegation, but rather banker Charles Dawes led it. The plan called for Germany to introduce new taxes and back its currency with gold, making it more difficult to devalue. In exchange for these concessions, the allies rescheduled reparation payments. To aid Germany in rebuilding and making payments, the United States extended loans to Germany. France evacuated the Ruhr Valley. The Dawes Plan temporarily averted disaster and allowed Germany to resume payments until 1929, when the system broke down again, requiring another renegotiation with the Young Plan. The Dawes Plan created an unhealthy circulation of money. Germany borrowed money from the United States, gave that money to France and Britain, who in turn used it to pay back loans to the United States. This is what Herbert Hoover believed caused the Great Depression.

Hoover correctly recognized the role World War I played in shaping the events that led to the crash and Whitney's walk out onto the trading floor to try to stop it. The events played out in the rarified air of high finance and diplomacy, but the changes could also be seen in the life of Charles Ponzi when he arrived in Boston.

The Ponzi Scheme

The Ponzi scheme is legendary, even more so since the arrest in late 2008 of Bernie Madoff for operating a $65 billion Ponzi scheme. Charles Ponzi did not invent the scam, but he took it to new heights. Madoff and Ponzi operated during times when Americans obsessed over wealth and investing had become a national pastime. Although compared to twenty-first-century America, few people invested in the stock market, but the twenties saw the stock market enter into the popular consciousness. The rising stock market combined with the emergence of a new economy made it seem easy to make a fortune. Following World War I Ponzi created the innocuously named Securities Exchange Company to deal in postal coupons. While it is possible that Ponzi might have intended to form a legitimate company, the reality is that his scheme would never work. It evolved into one of the largest Peter/Paul (where you take from Peter to pay Paul) scams in US history.

Charles Ponzi, an Italian immigrant, embodied the seedier side of the go-go ethos of the 1920s. Ponzi immigrated to the United States, in part, to put his criminal past behind him. However, he continued to run afoul of the law, being convicted of crimes in both the United States and Canada as he drifted before settling in Boston in 1920, where he embarked on his elaborate scam. That Ponzi promised easy riches made it easy to ignore those who raised red flags. Ponzi's scam seemed plausible because people wanted to believe in easy money.

Ponzi promoted the idea of taking advantage of the end of the gold standard to speculate in international currency using postal coupons. Before World War I, the gold standard facilitated international trade by establishing clear exchange rates in gold. One knew how much gold a US dollar, Russian ruble, or British pound would bring. However, people found gold difficult to physically deal in, so the major countries established postal coupons to serve as a convenient method of transferring money from one country to another. That is, a person would purchase the coupons in a post office in one country and redeem them in another nation's post office, thus smoothing international transactions. When, during the Great War, the international financial system went off the gold standard it became theoretically possible to speculate in currencies, because currencies could change value in relation to each other. A currency market existed. Ponzi argued he could buy coupons in Italy, redeem them in the United States, and make money based on the different exchange rates. Ponzi attracted customers by promising a 50 percent return on their investment in three months.

In the frenzy, investors in his Securities Exchange Company fell for an old trick. Ponzi transfixed Bostonians as a sharply dressed immigrant who made millions overnight and, seemingly, could do so for others. People eager to get rich quick ignored both common sense and the warnings of some journalists that his claims were too good to be true. They pointed out, among other things, that not enough postage exchange coupons existed for Ponzi to engage in millions of dollars' worth of speculation. Instead, Ponzi used money from new investors to pay previous investors. He robbed Peter to pay Paul. As long as he could attract enough investors to pay the maturing notes, his scheme could continue. As he built credibility a frenzy developed and people eagerly entrusted him with their life savings. In the process, Ponzi became a celebrity. His customers included prominent citizens and law enforcement officials. He promised charitable contributions, especially to charities serving immigrants. Eventually, Ponzi's scheme collapsed under the pressures of investigations and the need to sustain a sufficient number of new investors. His scheme did not necessarily foreshadow the collapse of the stock market, but it did point to the blurry line between investment and speculation. Ponzi took advantage of many of the same things that New Era boosters did.

The 1920s began and ended on a low note. The decade began with recession, violence, and fear. It ended with a major stock market crash. The years in between, however, were golden. When the economy hit its stride in the middle of the decade, everything looked different. Prosperity and progress seemed unstoppable. After the recession the economy grew at a brisk pace throughout the decade, which was marked by two mild recessions, one from May 1923 to July 1924 and another from October 1926 to November 1927. Gross National Product grew at a healthy 4.6 percent for the decade. During the boom New Era boosters talked of an old economy grounded in the industries of the nineteenth century. By contrast, boosters painted the New Era economy as modern, based on fast-flowing information, flashy new consumer goods, and free-flowing money. Republicans celebrated businessmen who seemed to be creating the technology, goods, and financing that fulfilled the promise of modernity. By the late 1920s, boosters proudly proclaimed that the economy might produce a virtual utopia—perhaps rivaling that promised by communism—in which investing in the stock market created a new form of investor democracy and the rising tide of prosperity would end poverty. In the next chapter we will see what that looked like.

2 How Business Culture Encouraged
Consumer Spending

William Jennings Bryan: Populist to Promoter

To DEMONSTRATE THE powerful allure of the New Era, consider
the Great Commoner, William Jennings Bryan. In July 1896 the junior congressman from Nebraska, Bryan, delivered his "Cross of Gold" speech at the
Democratic National Convention. He gave voice to the frustrations of rural
Americans unhappy with the emerging industrial and financial order. Bryan
embodied the Jeffersonian and Jacksonian populist tradition of distrusting
finance. His thunderous denunciation of the gold standard roused the delegates to nominate him for the presidency. Although Bryan lost in 1896, he
carried the crusade into the twentieth century, becoming one of the nation's
leading critics of the gold standard and the money trust. During the 1920s
Bryan would be best known as a cultural warrior championing the values of
rural Americans who felt threatened as more Americans moved to cities. By
the twenties for the first time a majority of Americans lived in urban areas.
In this newly urbanized America Bryan defended traditional rural, protestant
values and policies, such as Prohibition, against modernity.

Bryan did not join lost-generation writers like Ernest Hemingway, Sinclair Lewis, and F. Scott Fitzgerald in decrying the prevalent materialism of American culture. Deracinated expatriate writers swam against the current of American culture. For them the disappointments of the Great War led to alienation, but many Americans dealt with it by making money and shopping. Lewis's *Main Street* (1920) and *Babbitt* (1922) could not deflate the optimism of real civic boosters or puncture the romanticism of small towns. Fitzgerald's *The Great Gatsby* (1925) sold poorly during the twenties. After all in 1920 Americans elected Harding, a small-town booster who promoted small-town values, in a landslide. Republicans now rejected the trust-busting rhetoric of the Progressive Era. In contrast to Wilson and Roosevelt's administrations, Secretary of Commerce Hoover saw it as his job to facilitate cooperation between businesses. Enthusiasm for business innovation and consumer products stood at the heart of the New Era economy.

Not even the Great Commoner could resist the New Era hype. Bryan waged his fight against modernity not on the field of economics but in the culture wars. During the twenties Bryan made headlines for fighting the teaching of evolution in the Scopes Monkey Trial. By the early 1920s, however, Bryan had already begun selling real estate in south Florida. Real estate developers, led by Carl G. Fisher, built housing in Miami Beach, transforming the Everglades and southern Florida into a destination for refugees from northern winters. Fisher began in the bicycle business, but he made his first fortune in automobiles, providing headlights for the booming automobile industry. He then moved on to promoting races; he had a hand in building the Indianapolis Motor Speedway. Fisher, in an era before the government assumed the responsibility, also built roads. Fisher's road, the Dixie Highway, connected the Midwest to southern Florida. Thus started his interest in Florida real estate. Fisher promoted Florida much as he had promoted automobiles and roads. He purchased a giant, lighted billboard in Times Square bearing the message "It's June in Miami." Aggressive publicity, easy travel, and cheap credit made the Florida winters attractive and affordable, creating a real estate bubble. Like other promoters, Fisher began in manufacturing but by the twenties had migrated to investing and speculating.

Bryan did not need Fisher's urging to embrace Florida. He had already discovered the pleasures of Florida winters. Bryan's long career had brought him to southern Florida in 1912, when he and his wife purchased a winter home

When Thomas Edison, Harvey Firestone, and Henry Ford attended the funeral of President Warren G. Harding in Marion, Ohio, they paid respect to a president who helped set the tone for the 1920s by boosting business and introducing conservative economic policies. Harding oversaw the postwar shrinking of the national government and the introduction of policies friendly to business. Ironically, Edison, Firestone, and Ford represented what New Era boosters referred to as the old economy. When Harding died in office in 1923, Vice President Calvin Coolidge assumed the presidency and would oversee the boom known as the Coolidge Prosperity. *Source:* Ohio Historical Society (public domain).

there. After he resigned as Woodrow Wilson's secretary of state, among the causes Bryan took up in his final decade included Florida real estate, becoming one of several celebrities who boosted Florida. Bryan "flipped" his winter home for about half a million dollars. That, combined with his promotional work, made him a millionaire; his wealth made him defensive, given his lifelong politics.

In 1926, shortly after Bryan left for Dayton, Tennessee, to battle evolution, the Florida boom fizzled due to unforeseen and unfortunate incidents. Journalists began to question the wisdom of investing in the state. A dispute among railroad companies that led to a partial embargo of the state and a shipwreck blocked Miami Harbor, increasing doubts about Florida. Suddenly, but perhaps predictably, Florida did not look so attractive. Bryan would soon be dead, but his final years demonstrate that few could resist the lure of speculation.

As we saw at the end of the previous chapter, easy money tempted people in places other than Florida. Bostonians bought into Charles Ponzi's scheme, a much shakier proposition than Florida real estate. One can see the appeal of these opportunities. The economy improved. The stock market soared. Real estate prices increased. Boom industries, such as the automobile and the radio, drove the economic improvement. Why couldn't an Italian immigrant rise from nowhere by hitting upon a way to make a fortune in international currency speculation? Why shouldn't you buy Florida real estate? You vacation in Florida, in your car, driving on new roads. Bryan vouched for it. Many people wanted to make money now.

Is it fair to use Ponzi and Bryan as our introduction to the 1920s market? Perhaps not, but they did capture much of the flavor of the public's eagerness for new money-making opportunities. The Florida land bubble, and later the stock market bubble, demonstrate the difficulty in separating speculation from investment. Real and substantial changes to the economy made these bubbles seem credible and sustainable. The new, postwar economy had real opportunities and, despite the promises boosters made, real risks. Not all the financial wizards of the 1920s ran a scheme, but enough did that it helps account for the appearance of several bubbles and the market's collapse at the decade's end.

For the consumer economy to take hold, advertisers had to convince Americans to give up long-held beliefs in the value of thrift. Ben Franklin's old axiom that "a penny saved is a penny earned" would no longer serve. A penny saved did not increase economic growth. Self-improvement came not through self-denial but by purchasing the right products, a theme found in the advertising campaigns of the decade.

During the twenties the American dream did not evoke the Founding Fathers' agrarian republicanism or Bryan's Christian fundamentalism; commercialism underlay the new American dream. A man found his value in his bank account, not his character. During the New Era businesses produced a bounty of new products, new ways to buy, new reasons to buy, and new ways to make money.

Advertising

One historian has referred to advertising agents of the twenties as prophets of modernity. Intellectuals like Herbert Hoover might have been interested in the promise of scientific management and new forms of communication, but advertisers found in radio and glossy magazines a perfect way to tell Americans how to be successful, popular, sexy, and modern. Advertisers no longer just informed the public of available products, now businesses sought to control and shape markets. The maturing advertising industry taught Americans how to transition to a consumer-driven economy.

As mentioned in the previous chapter, World War I propaganda played a role in the maturation of advertising. Sophisticated techniques developed by the Committee for Public Information found their way into business, where they played a role in a larger shift in business culture. Professional business managers, who often did not come from a manufacturing background but rather studied management at a university, focused less on production and more on marketing to influence consumers' buying habits.

Albert Lasker, sometimes known as the father of modern advertising, pioneered shaping markets and altering social practices in the process. Lasker's influence could be seen in 1920, when the Republican Party picked him to sell its presidential candidate, Harding. Indeed, Lasker's work included opening markets for the New Woman, much as he addressed women voters in 1920. Lasker had worked his way up the corporate ladder to become the head of the firm Lord and Thomas. As part of a new breed of advertisers, Lasker used psychology to influence consumers.

Lasker set out to change social norms in such a way as to make new markets. Some of his more famous campaigns included making it acceptable for women to smoke in public, in the process doubling the number of potential customers. Lasker explained his campaigns in public terms. The double standard made it unfair that women could not enjoy smoking in a restaurant the same way that a man did. His advertisements stressed the benefits of smoking instead of eating candy, "To keep a slender figure, no one can deny . . . reach for a Lucky instead of a sweet." Advertisers targeted women by telling them that modern women smoked and wore cosmetics, therefore women needed to become consumers of these goods. Other products besides tobacco and sweets contributed to a better love life. Listerine cured "chronic halitosis," the bad breath that stood in the way of your success, in business or in dating. Fleischmann's yeast cured "intestinal fatigue." For young people looking to be modern, they had to look no farther than the pithy prose and striking images found in advertisements.

The advertising professionals had a vision of what society should be and how consumers fit into it. As advertising matured it became more sophisticated. Newly professionalized ad men and copy writers did more than tell shoppers about a product. They created desire. Rather than reflect reality, advertisements blended words and images depicting a fantasy world that people could aspire to achieve. Advertisements depicted ways of overcoming the barriers to achieving a life that people could aspire to but often was outside their grasp without going into debt. This could be better health, a perfect marriage, or a warm family. Advertisements did not depict working-class men and women; rather they portrayed a world of universal upper-class or ubiquitous but ill-defined middle-class status. If not a family with children, ads featured the young, urban, and sophisticated.

Lasker and others embodied a new trend in business that came into its own during the twenties. Companies merged product design, advertising, and function. Social science research would help determine what consumers wanted and, in turn, also used research to shape their desires. Some companies developed internal agencies, not content to hire outside agencies such as Lasker's pioneering advertising firm, Lord and Thomas. US Rubber and Swift Meats led the way in creating research marketing departments. Company leaders considered marketing, not just demand but how demand could be created, when designing a new product. By 1929 advertising had become a $3 billion business, a substantial portion of the cost of distributing a product. As happened elsewhere in the economy, the rise of one industry spurred on other businesses.

The decade saw the birth of the modern, glossy magazine filled with advertisements and stories aimed at busy people eager for self-improvement.

The world found in magazine advertisements featured middle-class people with highbrow, or at least middlebrow, aspirations. Obviously, people had been buying newspapers, dime novels, pulps, and the like for some time, but now magazines flourished in the realm between highbrow literary sophistication and lowbrow pulp titillation. Advice, gossip, and news filled the magazines. Celebrities graced the covers. So many magazines became available that DeWitt and Lila Wallace founded *Reader's Digest* in February 1922 as a magazine about magazines. *Reader's Digest* summarized the contents of other magazines in order to allow busy people to sample. With a similar idea Briton Hadden and Henry Luce founded *Time* in March 1923 as the first weekly news magazine in the country. They targeted busy, modern people who lacked the time to follow all the news. They kept the articles light and easy to read, often focusing on celebrities and politicians (as celebrity). *Time* magazine often focused on people, with the best example being the *Time* "Man of the Year." In 1927 Charles Lindbergh was named *Time*'s first Man of the Year in honor of his historic nonstop flight across the Atlantic to Paris.

The New Corporation

Advertisers had an abundance of goods to sell, produced by new companies but also by older companies. The 1920s saw a wave of consolidation; this time companies sought to decentralize management structures and diversify product lines. Over 5,000 mergers took place from 1925 to 1931. Industrial production became increasingly centered in a few large companies. In what historian Alfred Chandler refers to as the "visible hand" of management, these large companies began administering prices rather than having markets dictate prices. General Motors and General Electric stand as two good case studies of the trends. Both companies grew out of consolidation and were based on older technologies that came of age in the twenties. Both concentrated their economic power while decentralizing structure to allow them to operate in more markets.

New technologies combining with the maturation of older technologies seemed to justify the excitement of boosters. The electric power industry is an excellent example. Thomas Edison pioneered the commercial development of electricity in the 1880s. George Westinghouse entered the field using Nikola Tesla's alternating current. For a period of time, Edison's direct current competed with Westinghouse's alternating current. As so often happened, J. P. Morgan consolidated the electric industry by creating General Electric

(GE) in 1896. Morgan's consolidation, that is, "morganization," brought efficiencies of scale to a formally competitive industry. GE went on to become one of the original companies on the Dow Jones Industrial Average.

By the 1920s the electric industry, besides being a giant, consolidated business, had matured to the point where it transformed other parts of the economy. Prior to the adoption of electricity, a visitor to a factory would have found it a whirling, noisy, dirty place. Steam-powered engines drove elaborate systems of shafts and leather belts connecting the machinery. Before electric power, shafts and belts presented real dangers on a factory floor. Workers fed steam engines wood, charcoal, or (most commonly) coal that drove the shafts that drove the machinery. The belts could snap, or workers could get caught in them. The widespread availability of electricity, and electric motors, changed this. By eliminating the shaft and belt system, electricity streamlined the floor plans, making factories more efficient, cleaner, and safer. In 1914 electricity powered about 30 percent of manufacturing. By 1929, that figure increased to 70 percent, and steam engines disappeared from the American factory.

Not only did the factories seem new and modern, but they made the new consumer goods that transformed home life. By the middle of the decade, well over half of American homes had electricity powering new appliances and gadgets. GE and other companies sold shoppers vacuum cleaners, electric lights, washing machines, and refrigerators that made their homes more comfortable and easier to maintain. Sunbeam made electric irons that, along with washing machines, eased the burden of laundry day. By the end of the decade, the refrigerator had almost completely replaced the ice box. Previously, steam had powered refrigerators, but electricity made them quieter and efficient, much more something one wanted in a home, as GE advertisements made clear. Time freed from chores could be used for leisure. For entertainment Americans would listen to the radio, visit amusement parks, or go to the movies, all powered by electricity.

Entertainment

In the 1920s Hollywood emerged as a major center of business. The film industry shared with the electric industry a common background with Thomas Edison. Edison dominated the early film industry, but it had since matured beyond his grasp. In the process Hollywood became a symbol of the New Era. In 1915 President Woodrow Wilson watched D. W. Griffith's *The Birth of a Nation*. He offered his scholarly praise for the film, which celebrated the

Reconstruction Ku Klux Klan: "It is like writing history with lightning, and my only regret is that it is all so terribly true." With *The Birth of a Nation*, the first feature-length film, Griffith established the grammar of modern narrative cinema, revolutionizing the movie industry. The decade saw the film industry mature into a stable business on the West Coast, to the point where its location would become synonymous with business.

In 1923 Harry Chandler of the *Los Angeles Times* erected the now iconic "Hollywood" sign to promote real estate development. Film makers would take him up on it and transform his sign into an iconic symbol of the film industry. Although film companies still made use of other locations, such as New Jersey and Florida, the industry consolidated in Southern California to take advantage of the consistent sunshine and good weather and to escape the reach of East Coast lawyers. Edison had vigorously sued other companies for patent infringement. By the end of the decade over twenty Hollywood studios produced over 800 films. In 1927 the first talking film, *The Jazz Singer*, appeared. Feature films helped usher out the old nickelodeons, small theaters that charged a nickel for a ticket.

During the decade the studio system developed; it would exist through the 1950s. With the studio system, the companies (aka studios) approached film making as mass production, putting creative talent under long-term contracts. Studios adopted the assembly line as their model, making films on large production lots, looking for efficiencies from size and repetition. These integrated companies controlled all aspects of the industry, from production to distribution to viewing. The five major studios, Warner Brothers (1923), Famous Players–Lasky Corporation (1916) (which became Paramount in 1927), RKO, Loew's (later Metro-Goldwyn-Mayer), and Fox Film Corporation (later Twentieth Century Fox), integrated backward; they owned movie palaces and distribution companies that ensured their films would be seen. The Little Three Studios of Columbia Pictures, Universal Pictures, and United Artists competed with the Big Five Studios. There also existed many small, independent companies. Disney Studios, founded in 1923 by Roy and Walt Disney, which specialized in animation, would go on to be the best-known of these.

Hollywood glamour became a symbol of the twenties. Americans followed the exploits of the stars, often crafted by the advertising agents working for the studios. Moviegoers embraced the glamour of Hollywood. Americans dressed up for an evening to go to a movie palace to see the latest film. Especially for the middle class, seeing a movie highlighted an evening out. Although few thought of it this way, the palaces belonged to the chains of theaters affiliated with the studios. Theater owners hoped to use the palaces to attract middle-class people out on the town for an evening, the large companies shaping the markets with the visible hand of marketing and integration.

For those opting to stay home, increasingly that meant listening to the radio. When Warren G. Harding won the presidency in 1920, Pittsburgh radio station KDKA announced the results, the first time presidential election results were announced over the airwaves. However, not that many people heard the announcement because at the beginning of the decade, radios and radio stations remained a rarity. By the end of the decade, like film, the radio had arrived as a business and a mainstay of national and popular culture. Politicians now had to master the art of communicating over the radio. Furthermore, radio now created both an opportunity and a dilemma.

The Golden Age of Radio began in the 1920s and ran through the 1950s, giving Americans staples of popular culture such as soap operas and the Lone Ranger. While people would buy the radio, it was not obvious that the radio would become a centerpiece of the home, a piece of furniture that family and friends would gather around. Buying on installment became more acceptable because of the demand for radios. Homeowners needed electricity to operate the radio. But what about the airwaves over which the transmissions traveled? Who would own those? How would customers pay for the shows they enjoyed?

For business, making money on radio shows you gave away for free presented a problem (something that should be familiar to the Internet generation). To modern readers the obvious answer is advertising. This is obvious, however, in hindsight. Radio advertising evolved with the technology. Companies often sponsored an entire show rather than buying space for an advertisement. For example, one might listen to the A&P Gypsies, named after a sponsoring grocery store chain, or the Voice of Firestone, which was named after its sponsoring tire company. Soap operas, introduced in 1930, took their name from the soap companies that sponsored them. It took some time to develop the serialized programming paid for with advertisements that sought to convince the listening public to purchase their goods.

RCA (Radio Corporation of America), as the centerpiece company making the hot new technology, became the glamour stock of the decade. General Electric founded RCA, and it remained a division of GE until 1930. As with other developments of the twenties, RCA had its roots in World War I.

During the early days of the war, Germany destroyed the transatlantic telegraph cables of the belligerent nations, forcing them to communicate either through neutral nations or with other technologies such as radio. In 1917, when the United States entered the war, the federal government took over patents to harness radio for the war effort. With the end of the war, radio returned to private hands. The Army and Navy proposed to General Electric that it create a subsidiary that they would contract with for long-range radio equipment. GE consolidated a number of smaller firms into a publicly held company, with GE holding a majority share. During the 1920s RCA did not pay dividends. People invested in RCA stock purely on the expectation that it would continue to grow in value. RCA became the symbol of the emerging popular culture and the public fascination with the stock market.

If the radio allowed Americans a greater sense of interconnectedness, the automobile also contributed to the creation of mass culture. In 1900 Americans registered 8,000 cars; in 1929 the number stood at 23 million, not including trucks and buses. All those cars on the roads served as a catalyst for other changes. For one thing, motorists needed better and more roads. In 1916 Congress passed legislation enabling states to create highway departments. In 1921 Congress provided matching funds to build or maintain roads it deemed to be "primary." Congress also created the Bureau of Public Roads, which would plan a system of highways connecting cities with populations of greater than 50,000. By 1929 the United States had 3 million miles of roads.

The Business of America

Americans took to these roads in large numbers, bringing their new cars with them on vacations. Motor touring became popular, and the car became symbolic of freedom. Americans traveled to state and national parks to fish and camp. Vacationing and travel slowly but surely entered into the working- and middle-class cultures. Leisure travel was no longer the domain of the wealthy.

General Motors and Ford Motor Company stood at the vanguard of the automobile future. Until Henry Ford unveiled the Model T automobile in 1907 and began making it on an assembly line in 1913, automobiles were expensive toys for the wealthy. Henry Ford's contribution to modern America included making the automobile affordable for the masses.

Ford embodied both sides of the twenties, at once a pioneer in business innovation and a man whose intolerance limited his and his company's growth.

During World War I, in 1916, Henry Ford sponsored a peace ship to Europe, hoping to bring the Great War to an end. He turned the presidency of the company over to his son, Edsel, but remained the de facto leader of the company. During the decade, he became known for Fordism, building on the work of efficiency expert Frederick Taylor. Fordism emphasized minimizing the cost of the final product through mechanization, efficiency, and standardization. Ford's $5 day reflected his belief that consumerism, achieving a sufficient standard of living, would bring about peace and prosperity. However, in the years following World War I Ford seemed to have lost his visionary touch. He embraced mechanical efficiency but refused to embrace marketing and financial capitalism.

In the mid-1920s, as Ford was faced with increased competition, sales of the Model T slumped. He refused to modernize the car to meet consumer taste or to sell on credit, but eventually, in 1927, Ford conceded and replaced the Model T with the Model A. Ford shut down his assembly line for the conversion; the shutdown is credited for creating a mild recession. A populist distrust of Wall Street combined with anti-Semitism explains Ford's reluctance to embrace financial capitalism. Ford, a leading anti-Semite, encouraged his workers to join the Ku Klux Klan. He also financed the distribution of *The Protocols of the Elders of Zion*, an anti-Semitic tract that purported to uncover a Jewish plot for global domination, and "The International Jew: The World's Problem," in the *Dearborn Independent* (which Ford owned). As a result, the Ford Motor Company lost ground to more financially sophisticated rivals, particularly General Motors.

William C. Durant, founder of General Motors and Chevrolet, shared Ford's vision of mass production, but unlike Ford Durant embraced finance and consumerism. Ford came at it from manufacturing, relying on the power of mass production to give consumers a quality, affordable car. Ford, rather famously, said that a customer can have a Ford in any color he wants, as long as it is black. Durant, however, did not share Ford's flare for the mechanical. Ford lacked Durant's salesmanship. Durant understood that consumers wanted options and wanted their cars to reflect their social status. New makes and models heralded planned obsolescence. Designed to be easily repaired, a Model T stayed the same, never looking out of date or modern or fashionable. A GM car could look fashionable, and those driving last year's model felt pressure to get the new model.

This Studebaker advertisement from 1920 reflects the new way companies sold cars. An automobile was not just a form of transportation but part of a lifestyle. It "identifies you." Also, note that the advertisement depicts, and targets, young women as modern consumers. *Source:* Advertisement in *National Geographic* magazine, September 1920, via Wikimedia Commons (public domain).

Durant pioneered several innovations that Ford resisted. These included annual models, consumer financing, and offering multiple makes and models to fit different customer niches and incomes. Durant incorporated General Motors in 1908 and then acquired other car manufacturers, including Cadillac, Buick, Oldsmobile, and various suppliers. Thus he both horizontally and vertically integrated. However, Durant overextended himself financially and lost control of GM. In 1910 he partnered with Louis Chevrolet to form a new car company, eventually buying him out in 1914. Durant's success with Chevrolet enabled him to purchase shares of GM, regaining control of the company, at least temporarily. In 1920 the DuPont family interest gained control of GM, and in 1921 he launched Durant Motors. His real passion, however, remained playing the stock market; he lost his fortune in the crash, when he invested to demonstrate his confidence in Wall Street.

Alfred P. Sloan continued Durant's innovations but added stability to the company. Sloan had been the president and owner of Hyatt Roller Bearing Company, which became part of United Motor Company, where Sloan worked with Durant. General Motors purchased United Motor Company, and Sloan joined GM. Sloan rose to the presidency of General Motors in 1923. As the head of GM, he oversaw the decentralization of the company, which allowed it to compete in several markets. At the same time, Sloan contributed to the transformation of business, from focusing on production to creating markets. Companies wanted to find new ways to encourage consumers to buy their products.

During the 1920s, Sloan made GM into the largest manufacturer of cars in the world through an emphasis on statistical management and by extending Durant's ideas. Sloan's emphasis on annual styling of models led the way to planned obsolescence. GM also offered cars at various prices, which allowed customers to climb the success ladder. A consumer would enter the market buying a Chevrolet, but as he or she met with success future cars might include Pontiacs, Oldsmobiles, Buicks, and Cadillacs.

One cannot overstate the impact of the rise of the automobile industry and the importance of the success of the mass production of the automobile. The car transformed American society and created many related industries. For example, with the rise of cars came a new demand for tires. B. F. Goodrich made Akron, Ohio, the "Rubber Capital of the World." Harvey Firestone's Firestone Tire and Rubber Company had made tires and parts for buggies, but he used his friendship with Henry Ford to become a key supplier for the Ford Motor Company. Both Goodrich and Firestone benefited from the rise of the automobile. State and local governments placed a new emphasis on building paved roads, which served as a subsidy for the trucking industry. Railroads complained bitterly about what they perceived as an unfair subsidy. With better roads and cars, more Americans moved to the suburbs. Cars and good roads made it easier to work in one place and live in another. Cars also became part of the recreational fabric of the nation. People joined motor clubs and traveled around the country.

Labor

Although neither boosters nor critics would admit it, the new American dream was neither as golden nor as empty as they made it out to be.

As we have seen, workers found Henry Ford's $5 day, implemented in 1914, something of a double-edged sword. As the company prospered Ford employees could earn enough to indulge in the new consumer culture, buying Model Ts, but they also gave up an element of freedom as the company's Social Services division inspected their private lives to see if they deserved the $5 day. Ford famously opposed unionization. Similarly, Calvin Coolidge praised business and urged workers to be good employees. He equated going to work in a man's business to going to worship in a church. He was, however, not so generous with labor. Coolidge's rise to the presidency began when he fired striking Boston policemen in 1919. According to Coolidge, police had no right to strike against the public good. The Boston police strike symbolized a general decline in the fortunes of organized labor following World War I. Organized labor had prospered during the war, in part because of the American Federation of Labor's no-strike pledge and Samuel Gompers's partnership with the Wilson administration. From 1915 to 1920 trade union membership almost doubled, but labor's good fortune would not last. The end of the war brought a loss of government sanction. The failed strikes, the Red Scare, and the recession of 1920 dealt organized labor a blow. The trend continued, and in the early 1920s strikes in the coal and railroad industries went poorly for workers.

The West Virginia Coal Wars, in 1920–21, have assumed mythic proportions in literature, songs, poems, and movies. The Coal Wars consumed southern West Virginia, pitting thousands of miners against the coal companies and their allies. The strike began with a shootout at Matewan, West Virginia, between miners and Baldwin-Felts agents. It raged through the mountains until it culminated in the Battle of Blair Mountain, one of the largest insurrections since the Civil War, involving over 10,000 striking miners fighting a combination of Baldwin-Felts detectives, county sheriff deputies, state police, and US Army forces. To this day the battle is remembered, in part, because of the use of air power against a civilian population in the United States. Although coal company planes dropped the ordnance, the myth persists that the US Army Air Force bombed the miners. The strikes ultimately failed, and the West Virginia government tried the strike leaders for treason.

The coal companies won the coal wars, but tension and violence that gripped the coal fields of southern West Virginia represented long-standing problems. Commentators on the economy considered the coal industry part of the "old" economy and a sick industry. As with agriculture, mechanization had increased efficiency but had also created downward pressure on wages and profits. Fewer workers could mine more coal, but machines cost a lot of money. Although still a widely used form of energy, coal faced competition from oil, natural gas, and electricity. Electric power plants used coal, but more Americans opted to warm and light their homes with these cleaner energy sources.

The second substantial strike that challenged the Harding administration came in another old industry, the railroads. As with the coal industry, the problems in the railroad industry had been forming for some time. During the late nineteenth and early twentieth centuries, the railroad industry had been troubled. Because of high capital costs and intense competition from each other and the emergence of the trucking industry, railroad executives cried foul. From their point of view, trucking benefited from an unfair subsidy in the form of paved roads. The railroad business struggled before the United States entered World War I and buckled under the stress of mobilization.

To increase railroad efficiency during mobilization, the government nationalized the railroads under the US Railroad Administration directed by Secretary of the Treasury William McAdoo. The Wilson administration oversaw one of the largest experiments in nationalization in US history. Congress promised that the railroads would be returned to the original owners, but when the war ended a debate ensued over the fate of the railroads, and in 1920 the government returned them to private ownership. However, Congress passed the Railroad Transportation Act, which gave the Interstate Commerce Commission increased regulatory power over the railroads.

The railroads formed the lifeline of the economy. When railroads stopped running, the rest of the economy slowed down, dramatically. The railroad strike of 1922 grew out of wage cuts. Workers appealed the wage cuts to the Railroad Labor Board, which had been created in the 1920 act. When neither side would agree to arbitration, Attorney General Harry Daugherty obtained the first-ever nationwide injunction against the strikers from Chicago judge James Wilkerson. Following the injunction, the strike died a slow death.

The postwar years proved a setback to the gains labor unions had made during the war. Samuel Gompers, long-time president of the American Federation of Labor who had worked with the Wilson administration, died in 1924. His successor, William Green, promoted management-labor cooperation but with limited success. Green advocated cooperation with business to find compromises on wages and hours that would benefit both sides. Cooperation or confrontation, organized labor did not do well during the twenties.

During the 1920s businesses used several tactics to combat unions. As we saw with the coal industry, these tactics included violence. Business leaders promoted the American Plan, arguing that open shops were American and closed shops were un-American, a tactic that echoed the fear of communism and socialism from the first Red Scare. Companies required workers to sign contracts swearing not to join a union. Other companies sought to create a more benign image through welfare capitalism, under which a company provided benefits to build loyalty and remove worker motivation for joining a union. Welfare capitalism could range from sponsoring a sports team to a company union. From 1920 to 1925 the number of company unions in the United States went from 145 to 432. Henry Ford's $5 day is an example of welfare capitalism. Eligible workers over the age of twenty-two who worked eight-hour days would receive the high wages. The Sociology Department, an agency within the company, administered the program, determining if a worker met the criteria of being sober, industrious, and upright.

While labor unions fared poorly, the overall labor force matured, and unemployment was low. From 1923 to 1929 the average unemployment rate was 3.3 percent.[1] Several things need to be considered. The low unemployment rate coincided with a growing gap between the rich and the poor that eventually undermined the increasing consumer demands of the period. Several government policies helped retain jobs. A high tariff protected domestic industries. The immigration restriction laws of 1921 and 1924 decreased the number of immigrants. The 1920 census shows that for the first time a majority of Americans lived in urban areas. The number of women in the workforce increased, especially in feminized occupations like teaching and nursing. That, combined with the sexual revolution and increased access to birth control, led to a decrease in the birthrate. The twenties saw the rise of the professions and occupations needed to make corporate America run.

Despite the uneven nature of the prosperity, Americans felt good about themselves as the decade came to a close. Surely the rising economic tide would eventually float those left behind. Organized labor could join with the prosperous corporation in company unions. Farmers would eventually do better. Everyone would find a way to get ahead in the New Era. Perhaps no better statement of New Era boosterism exists than Herbert Hoover's acceptance of the Republican nomination in 1928: "We in America today are nearer to the final triumph over poverty than ever before in the history of any land." Soon, Hoover predicted, the poorhouse would be a thing of the past. Hoover echoed other New Era boosters; the business cycles of old had disappeared. In hindsight we know this was not true. The booster optimism enabled the bubble that developed in the stock market during the late twenties.

Of course, the economy did change, and yes, the country did know prosperity, but all of this is tainted by the knowledge that the Great Depression would follow. History turned Hoover's optimistic campaign boosterism into irony. Hoover's name would not be associated with permanent prosperity but with Hoovervilles, shantytowns of the unemployed. To be fair to Hoover, just as predicting the decade of growth might have been difficult, few at the end of 1928 would have predicted that the nation would experience a decade of economic despair. Hoover could have used his nomination speech to warn the public about the dangers of speculating with borrowed money, but that would have brought him few votes and public ridicule.

3 How the Market Grew Bullish

The Coolidge Prosperity and the Investor's Democracy

THANKS TO THE EFFORTS of bankers and boosters, the twenties saw investing in stocks go from Wall Street to Main Street. During the Bull Market of the 1920s, politicians cheered on the stock market as serving both the private and the public, a rising tide lifting all boats. Presidents Harding, Coolidge, and Hoover all boosted the new order. For them, the booming stock market justified their faith in the efficiency and modernity of business. The stock market offered the average citizen the opportunity to invest in America's business. As the historian Julia C. Ott has written, "During the Great Bull Market of the late 1920s, distributors of the corporate stock established and promulgated core economic precepts of modern conservatism. The ideology of shareholder democracy embedded in Jazz Age stock marketing did not, at first, reflect the existence of a sizable class of corporate shareholders."[1] The twenties saw Thomas Jefferson's dream of a commonwealth championed by populists like William Jennings Bryan wed to Alexander Hamilton's financial creation.

The rich got richer, but so did everyone else, or so the argument went.

By the end of the decade the Progressive Era warnings of the power of the money trust had given way to the argument that "everybody ought to be rich." However, the promise of investment did not spread wealth democratically throughout society, feeding into a gap between those who invested in the new democracy and those who did not invest. When Americans went to the polls, they sided with the financiers, possibly hoping to get a piece of the action. Critics of Wall Street found that during the 1920s the public's interest in denouncements of the money trust had dwindled; public opinion seemed to consider being a Wall Street tycoon a good thing. That political leaders not only ignored but cheered on the speculation helped create a speculative bubble. However, not everyone understood what they bought when they purchased stocks. The stock market bubble that burst in 1929 spoiled the idea of ending the poorhouse that Hoover had laid out when accepting the Republican presidential nomination. As the Founding Fathers understood, there can be a fine line between mob mentality and mass democracy.

To understand how Wall Street worked, we need to understand not only the mechanics of the markets but also who operated the markets. Who were the bankers that Americans celebrated? The stock market is best understood as a combination of mechanics and psychology. In this chapter, we look at how Wall Street functioned during the decade, with a focus on identifying when the stock market shifted from sound growth to a speculative bubble and what caused it. The New Era thinking of the 1920s fits the classic model of a bubble, complete with the argument that this time was different and only a fool would not take advantage of the rising market. If you weren't rich, you had no one to blame but yourself.

The Investing Public

From its inception, Wall Street had been ruled by a club of gentleman bankers, although upstarts, from time to time, challenged to get a seat at the table. During this decade of Republican rule, gentleman bankers found close ties to the government, often acting as diplomats, as we saw with the Dawes and Young Plans. At the same time, the traditional world of eastern bankers changed as average people began to follow and invest in the stock markets, creating a popular culture around the ticker tape, the investor's democracy. New Era boosters often compared buying a car on installments with buying a stock on margin, with the idea that stocks would make money, unlike a car. The investor democracy, however, never achieved a majority. During the

This illustration of the South Sea Bubble from Mackay's book shows what Livermore understood but many forgot during the twenties: bubbles are nothing new, and they will pop. Mackay's book is often referenced when studying speculation and bubbles. *Source:* Scanned from reprint of 1841/1852 editions of *Extraordinary Popular Delusions and the Madness of Crowds* by Charles Mackay, via Wikimedia Commons (public domain).

boom, the percentage of the population invested in the market rose from the single digits to about a quarter of the population. While not a majority, it was a significant increase. Perhaps more importantly, average people had access to credit and could use it to buy consumer goods, automobiles, or stocks and bonds. More so than at any previous time, average people's investments fueled the Bull Market. Brokers and bankers changed their practices to accommodate new investors, and, regardless of their status as investors, more people indulged in the "ticker tape" culture than ever before. The ticker tape became an object of public fascination and a symbol of the Coolidge Prosperity rather than simply a useful tool for financial traders.

People turned their attention to what had been, for the most part, a concern of a section of businesspeople. Prior to the twenties, if the public paid attention to Wall Street it was to scorn the bankers. On the most basic level the financial sector is a place where companies can seek out investors to help finance their firms. To accomplish this, companies sell stocks and bonds. As we saw with the Liberty Bonds, a bond is a security issued in exchange for a loan; in other words bonds represent debt for the bond issuer. For this reason, bonds can be issued by private companies as well as governments. The bond issuer will pay the bond owner interest for the use of his or her money. A stock is when a firm sells an ownership portion, or equity, to investors to raise funds.

The transformation in the popular attitude toward investing began during World War I. The US government borrowed money to finance the war, partly through popular bond drives. Selling the American people bonds raised money and served as propaganda. Movie stars, such as Douglas Fairbanks and Mary Pickford, urged Americans to buy Liberty Bonds. Fairbanks and Pickford were huge celebrities. Fairbanks appeared before a massive rally on Wall Street. Charlie Chaplin made the short film *The Bond* (1918) to encourage people to buy bonds. In the movie, Chaplin plays with the meaning of "bond," foreshadowing the materialism that would follow the war. While a bond could be one of friendship or love, the war made the Liberty Bond the most important "bond." Patriotism motivated Americans to become familiar with investing through purchasing bonds and accepting Wall Street as a place to make money for the good of the country.

While Americans became more comfortable with the idea of investing in Liberty Bonds, changes underway in the financial markets also made it easier to invest. Around the time of the First World War, companies changed the way they financed expansion. Prior to the war, if a company lacked cash it paid for expansion by issuing bonds. For example, J. P. Morgan and Company dealt mostly in the bond market (as it did during World War I) and only entered the stock market later.

Stocks became more attractive when, in April 1920, the Supreme Court declared that stock dividends did not qualify as income under the Sixteenth Amendment. In 1920 public companies—companies not privately owned by individuals or partners—offered two types of stocks, common and preferred. Preferred stock paid a fixed regular dividend with a greater claim on company assets in case of failure, but the owner had no voting rights in the company. Holders of common stock received irregular dividends, depending on company performance, and they had voting rights. Companies now looked to pay for expansion by withholding earnings from dividend payments, so companies started to pay smaller dividends on common stocks. Companies began issuing new stocks in place of a dividend; companies could raise money by issuing new offerings to stockholders. Companies now had a reason to sell stocks to the general public as more of the public had access to credit and exposure to the markets.

During and after the war, loose credit and easy money made the stock market more attractive. As a result call loans became more popular than the conservative time loans. With a time loan a person borrowed for a period of three months to a year with 20 percent collateral required from the borrower. A call loan covered one day with the option to renew, or not, with little or no collateral requirements. In other words, a lender had the daily option of calling in the debt, and the purchased stock often served as the collateral. Speculators who bought on margin favored call loans. This type of investing is done with leverage, one of the key concepts of the 1920s stock markets (or today's market). Leverage is when a person or a company uses debt to finance investment. A firm that is highly leveraged is one that has a high level of debt in comparison to equity in assets.

Debt financed much of the Bull Market. In 1920 brokers' loans consisted of $1 billion, in 1926 the amount reached $2.5 billion, and by October 1929 brokers made $8.5 billion in loans. Many of the new investors bought on margin. When buying on margin a person would pay the margin but borrow the rest from a broker. For example, if a person purchased a stock valued at $100 while putting down $10 (or 10%), he or she would owe the brokerage the remaining $90, often a call loan. If the stock went up in value, the buyer could realize a large return. A 10 percent increase in the value would result in a stock worth $110, which would be 100 percent of the amount invested (the original $10). However, if the stock went down in value it would be just as easy for the investor to be wiped out. A 10 percent reduction in the stock value would eliminate the original amount invested, resulting in a call for additional margin, that is, the borrower would have to put up more of his or her own cash. If the investor did not provide more cash for the margin, the broker or bank could force him or her to sell the stock. If the invested money came from a call loan, and the lending firm demanded that the loan be repaid, it could spell financial disaster.

Innovations in banking and technology made it possible for the average American to take advantage of financial dealings that had once only been available to a select few. Although Americans turned a jaundiced eye toward ideals of the Progressive Era political reforms, for the middle class technological innovation combined with prosperity to create a deep faith in progress, not through good government, but through private enterprise and technology. Business, epitomized by Wall Street, would lead to progress. "Modernity" is a word often associated with the twenties, and changes to the stock market and finance made it seem a part of the emergence of something new and exciting in the postwar years. So when Americans went to invest, where did they go? The rise of branch banking and brokerages only increased the public's fascination with Wall Street, as it increased access to financial services. You might buy and sell in the Midwest, but you watched Wall Street.

The Street

Wall Street, approximately eight city blocks long, is an address in New York City on the lower end of Manhattan that makes up the financial district. However, when people say "Wall Street," they may or may not literally mean this neighborhood. Sometimes they mean it as a metaphor for all of American finance. While we often see this shorthand, the New York Stock Exchange (NYSE) has not been the only market, either in the country or in New York City. Most major cities have a financial district. In Chicago, for example, the financial district is called the Loop. Wall Street itself hosted several markets. In the 1920s, 91 major banks called Wall Street home. Beyond the banks, 25 trust companies, 130 railroads, hundreds of insurance companies of various stripes, and a multitude of other finance-related businesses could be found on Wall Street. The Curb Exchange was located on Broad Street, just off Wall Street. On the Curb Exchange, as its name suggested, traders worked on the street, lacking the infrastructure and institutions of the Stock Exchange. New companies not ready for the NYSE went to the Curb Exchange for start-up money. Throughout its history, Wall Street has been home to the NASDAQ, the NYSE AMEX Equities (formerly the American Stock Exchange and before that the Curb Exchange), the New York Board of Trade, and others. Referring to this as "Wall Street" simplifies a baffling array of shifting names and changing characters. In recent years, globalization and technological changes have further deemphasized the location of the financial district, even more so turning "Wall Street" into the generic brand name for American finance.

During the 1920s the public became investors, and banking changed. Prior to this development, Wall Street had a "clubby" feel to it, as bankers viewed themselves as gentlemen and Wall Street as a place where character and connections counted. Richard Whitney belonged to this club. These gentleman bankers, noted for their conservatism, relied on personal connections and ties to European finance, specifically London. Discretion, formality, and confidentiality were the order of the day. Bankers considered government oversight an alien concept. Bankers, always in jacket and tie, worked in open offices at rolltop desks.

Few things exemplified this better than 23 Wall Street, the home of J. P. Morgan and Company. Construction began on the new building in 1913, the same year J. P. Morgan Sr. died. This iconic building became known as the "corner" and is now registered as a national historic site. A person strolling down Wall Street would see no sign identifying it as the home of a leading international bank. One did not walk in the door to open an account. J. P. Morgan and Company invited customers and did not lightly accept new ones. It did nothing as crass as advertise, even in the decade that saw the birth of modern advertising. Morgan brought both customs from London.

You would find no greater Anglophile than J. P. Morgan. J. P. Morgan's father, Junius Spencer Morgan, made his fortune as a partner of George Peabody, an American who operated his bank, George Peabody and Company, in London. Peabody, among other things, served as a broker for state governments, floating bonds in the London markets. Upon Peabody's death Morgan assumed control of the business, changing its name to J. S. Morgan and Company. J. P. Morgan, his son, inherited the company and modeled his bank on the prominent European banks. Morgan and his associates subscribed to what Ron Chernow has described as the "Gentleman Banker's Code." Chernow writes that "banks did not try to scout out business or seek new clients but waited for them to arrive with proper introductions. They had no branch offices and refused to take on new companies unless they first consulted with the former banker." Bankers wanted to avoid open competition, which also meant no advertising, no price competition, and no raiding of other firms' clients.[2] As we saw with our discussion of the Panic of 1907, it is not too wild an exaggeration to picture a group of prominent bankers meeting in J. P. Morgan's library to solve a crisis or strike a deal over bourbon and cigars. For most of Morgan's career, his connections to London and Europe paved the way to success. Partners considered the New York office as the inferior station to the London office. However, that would change.

As a private citizen, Morgan had been at the fulcrum of the balancing act between private and public interest. He had served as both a private banker and an unofficial central banker, so it is no wonder that Morgan became a symbol of financial capitalism. Morgan, while wealthy, was not the richest man in America. Indeed, upon Morgan's death, steel magnate Andrew Carnegie expressed surprise that Morgan's wealth amounted to only tens of millions and not hundreds of millions. Morgan invested a great deal of wealth in his massive, and impressive, art collection, so much so that his son had to liquidate some of it to meet the obligations in his estate. More than sheer personal wealth, Morgan's ability to access London and European financial markets to organize a deal made him powerful. He organized financial rescues, stabilized markets, and consolidated businesses. For many people, for good or ill, Morgan represented the face of trusts and the money monopoly.

When Morgan died, he left his business and his position to his son, also J. P. Morgan but known as Jack. The public perception of the two men blurred. Along with his father's wealth and position, Jack Morgan inherited his appearance. Their resemblance made it that much easier to conflate the two men. Amiable, shy, and competent, the younger Morgan liked yachting and lacked his father's ability to set national policy when it came to matters of finance and industry. The relative decline of the old guard came, in part, because of the success of bankers, like the elder J. P. Morgan, in rationalizing the economy and eliminating destructive competition. Jack Morgan lived in the financial world that his father, and men like him, built. Whereas the elder Morgan personally dominated his business, the younger Morgan built a strong organization of highly competent partners. While his personal power seemed diminished, the power of his company grew.

J. P. Morgan and Company served the needs of fellow businessmen and bankers. Investment banks were involved in financing companies or governments, and they underwrote and distributed securities, mostly bonds, for them. Investment banks financed mergers and acquisitions. They did not directly sell securities, but rather functioned as wholesalers distributing to brokers. Commercial banks had individual accounts and provided a variety of services. Commercial banks, in theory, had a responsibility to engage in conservative lending to protect the interest of depositors. While J. P. Morgan and Company practiced a variety of forms of banking, it primarily focused on investment banking. On Wall Street, a small community, prestige and gossip mattered. As we will see, its insular and opaque nature did not always serve it well. To average citizens looking in at Wall Street, recognizing these distinctions would have been difficult, if not impossible.

J. P. Morgan ran his bank as a partnership rather than a corporation, although it oversaw the creation of many large corporations and Morgan partners sat on many of their boards. Morgan partners earned a base salary of $1 million, but their real wealth came from their share of the company. As a partnership, all power rested with J. P. Morgan, who could dismiss a partner at will. Unlike a corporation, shareholders did not compel J. P. Morgan and Company to divulge information regarding its books or its transactions to shareholders or directors. Morgan and his partners assumed a patrician position in the economy. Morgan partners were cut from a specific social cloth, approaching something akin to an aristocratic noblesse oblige. To their critics, this blurring of their welfare with the national welfare presented a problem. Instinctively conservative, they attended the exclusive boarding schools and Ivy League universities, like Harvard and Yale, and they joined the right men's clubs. Social standing determined the Wall Street pecking order, a kind of informal separation by background and religion. They looked down upon the financial buccaneer, the speculator, almost as much as they looked down on Jews and Catholics.

While today J. P. Morgan is still a recognized name, the Morgan name did not stand alone in the public's association with Wall Street. Many of the big financial names of the 1920s have disappeared as banks have morphed and merged into huge financial institutions, but their legacy lives on. Kuhn, Loeb, and Company (later absorbed into Lehman Brothers) stood behind only J. P. Morgan as the second most prestigious Wall Street firm. Historian Maury Klein writes, "Kuhn, Loeb was the flagship from the German Jews in Wall Street, the most successful of whom grew quite as rich as their WASP rivals but were shunned socially. Anti-Semitism had been the way of life on Wall Street since the arrival of the first Jews and tended to become rampant during panics, when scapegoats were needed."[3] Solomon Loeb founded the company right after the Civil War, in 1867, but Jacob Schiff, a German-born Jew who joined the company in 1870, became the most famous partner. Schiff, who died in 1920, worked with E. H. Harriman on financing railroads. After

Schiff's death in 1920, Otto Kuhn and Felix Warburg ran the company. Merrill Lynch was known as the Catholic firm. Lehman Brothers and Goldman Sachs were Jewish firms. Dillon, Read, and Company dates back to the 1830s but gained prominence during the 1920s, when Clarence Dillon arranged the rescue of the Goodyear Tire & Rubber Company and the sale of Dodge Motor Company to Chrysler. The company oversaw the largest-ever stock offering in 1926. Critics incorrectly painted the financial district as a monolith. Whatever social differences existed among these older bankers, they did not result in differences of business practices.

The Gentleman Banker's Code did not apply to the bankers who embraced branch banks and open competition and began to outpace the investment banks in size if not in prestige. Charles E. Mitchell provided a contrast to J. P. Morgan. "Sunshine Charlie," as he was known, stood out among the boosters of the Bull Market and the New Era economy. He began his career with the Western Electric Company and the Trust Company of America. He operated his own firm for a few years and then joined National City Company. In 1921 National City Bank elected him president. Under his leadership, National City expanded with branch offices throughout the world but also engaged in the reckless speculation that led to the stock market crash. During the Great Depression Mitchell would be singled out for being responsible for the crash. Despised after the investigations regarding the crash, Mitchell eventually rebuilt his career. In the long term, he correctly gauged the future of the banking business, and while he showed poor judgment he was not among the worst of the schemers.

The Schemers

When Ivar Kreuger came to the United States from Sweden in the early 1920s looking for easy money, he went to the right place. Money sloshed through Wall Street. Kreuger is now famous as a financial schemer; a man who ran an international Ponzi scheme and whose reputation as a con artist is perhaps second only to Charles Ponzi's. Kreuger understood his status as the ultimate outsider, but his success in working with Wall Street and the investing public demonstrated the changes to the financial system. Kreuger began his dealings aboard an ocean liner crossing the Atlantic, thanks to its newly installed trading rooms, complete with telegraphs and ticker tape machine. He represented not only the potential for abuse, the seemingly too-good-to-be-true promise of fast riches, but also the transition from manufacturing to finance, albeit shady finance. Kreuger represented the other side of Morgan's code of the gentleman banker.

However shady his dealings became, Kreuger's began in legitimate businesses, matches and construction. Matches were a household necessity that people used regularly for lighting fires and lamps. Men carried matches. However, manufacturing inexpensive matches produced a slim profit margin. Kreuger's family ran a small match-manufacturing business in Sweden, but as a young man Ivar rejected working in the family business and opted instead to become an engineer. He had a successful career in the United States and Latin America, cofounding the construction firm Kreuger and Toll, which became an international success and made him a wealthy man. Kreuger and Toll made its mark by guaranteeing completion dates, switching the risk of delays from the client to the contractor. Kreuger and Toll evolved into a financial holding company that became the cornerstone of his empire. Unlike Herbert Hoover, who had a similar story of international business success, Kreuger did not turn to public service with his fortune in hand. Instead, as we have seen, Kreuger killed himself, ruined and in disgrace.

After World War I, Kreuger rejoined the family business, expanding it to form Swedish Match. His new company increased profits with government-sanctioned monopolies and product innovation. Swedish Match manufactured "safety matches," made with red phosphorous that did not accidentally ignite, like yellow phosphorous. Kreuger eventually acquired a government-sanctioned monopoly on match production in Sweden, Norway, and Finland, solving his problems with slim profits. In 1923 he founded International Match Corporation to expand outside of Europe, including the Americas. However, Kreuger's attempt to expand into the US market failed. The Diamond Match Company dominated the market and did not want to strike a deal. Kreuger's techniques of agreeing on market shares and government-sponsored monopolies were illegal in the United States under antitrust laws. Still, International Match Corporation controlled about 75 percent of the global market. Although Kreuger's attempt to make inroads into the US match market failed, he hit upon another idea.

Kreuger would take advantage of the economic difficulties of European nations to advance his match empire, thus earning him the nickname the "Match King." As the consummate outsider, Kreuger pitched the idea to Wall Street of investing in European monopolies. While the United States prohibited monopolies, European nations did not. Kreuger would arrange loans for cash-strapped European nations. In exchange, European governments would grant International Match a monopoly. To get the amount of money needed to finance his scheme, he turned to Wall Street. Americans could speculate in his venture, betting that the European monopolies would be profitable and that European nations could pay back the loans.

Kreuger's venture has been described as a Ponzi scheme, which is not altogether accurate. Like Ponzi, Kreuger argued that money could be made by taking advantage of the postwar situation. While this isn't technically necessary for a Ponzi scheme, the postwar debts did add credibility to Kreuger's claims. Kreuger created complicated international shell companies that allowed him to hide money. He attracted new investors by promising, and paying, 25 percent returns. The returns meant that his companies had to show a greater profit, which they failed to do, but he covered this loss by using hidden slush funds taken from new investors. In this aspect, he ran a Ponzi scheme. Kreuger could maintain his empire only by attracting new investors based on the payments taken from slush funds. Unlike Ponzi, Kreuger did have legitimate businesses, including a money-losing interest in the film industry (an interest he shared with Joseph Kennedy). Kreuger funded Swedish actress Greta Garbo's early films, which introduced her to Hollywood. Kreuger's construction and match-manufacturing companies made products and turned a legitimate profit; it simply did not provide enough to fund his ambitions. He did intend, and attempted to, operate his loans for monopolies scheme by robbing Peter to pay Paul in the interim. Although Kreuger raised some suspicion—Wisconsin officials attempted to investigate his activities—his operations were too large for a single state to successfully regulate or investigate. Kreuger's scheme unraveled with falling prices and shrinking markets during the Great Depression.

While scam artists like Kreuger and Ponzi enjoyed a period of public goodwill before their deception became known, other traders were notorious bears and pool operators. Jesse Livermore gained fame as a bear who made a fortune short selling during the Panic of 1907. Livermore's background did not foreshadow his success in finance; he did not fit the Wall Street mold. He began his career as a teenager working at Paine Webber in Boston, posting prices. While there he began placing bets in a bucket shop, a place where one could gamble on the prices of stocks. He moved to New York City, where he began working in legitimate stocks. He then lost that fortune betting on cotton futures and declared bankruptcy. Livermore made a second fortune during World War I and became a player in the stock market during the 1920s.

He advised investors not to hold onto stocks and not to listen to other people. When he lost fortunes, as he did, he blamed it on not listening to his own advice. During the twenties his bear market views did not take hold with the public. Short selling is when a broker sells an asset that he or she has borrowed from a third party. The seller plans on buying the asset back at a later date and returning it. It is a bet that the asset will drop in value, allowing the short seller to make a profit minus whatever fee the short seller gives the third party for use of the asset. If the asset increases in value, the short seller loses money. It is because short sellers are betting on a decline that gives them a poor reputation. Their desire for a bear market makes them a target of public wrath during panics. Some speculators engaged in "bear attacks," attempts to drive down the price of a stock of an otherwise healthy company. Sometimes an investor will counter a bear attack by cornering the market on a stock, forcing the price higher. Beyond the obvious critique that short sellers are taking advantage of misfortune or are destructive, short selling can take on a dynamic of its own, forcing stock prices into a downward spiral. Defenders of short selling argue that it is a necessary corrective, a market force to keep stocks from being overvalued. Livermore understood the mass psychology of markets and bubbles. As noted before, he enjoyed Charles Mackay's *Extraordinary Popular Delusions and the Madness of Crowds*.

The Upstarts

Joseph Kennedy epitomized the outsiders who challenged Wall Street's old guard in the twenties and went on to respectability. Today, Joseph Kennedy is best known as the father of President John Kennedy and patriarch of the political Kennedy family. Kennedy came from a Boston Irish Catholic family, the type of family old Wall Street insiders thought of as police men or laborers. Joseph Kennedy would go on to make a fortune on Wall Street and use that fortune to enter politics. In 1919 Kennedy joined a Wall Street firm. In 1923 he formed his own firm, where he invested heavily in the film industry, making money reorganizing Hollywood studios, merging several to create RKO Studios. Joseph Kennedy's work creating RKO fit the times. In 1920 the Supreme Court ruled that US Steel did not need to be broken up under the Clayton Antitrust Act, opening the door for a wave of second-tier mergers.

The statue of George Washington overlooking the financial district brings home the tension, and interplay, between older republican ideals and modern capitalism. Distrust of banks was a common theme in American politics before the 1920s, yet Washington's administration did much to encourage the creation of banks.
Source: Milstein Division of United States History, Local History and Genealogy, The New York Public Library, Astor, Lenox and Tilden Foundations (public domain).

While many of the great companies had been made during the age of "morganization," mergers now swept through newer, and smaller, industries such as film, banking, and utilities.

His fortune made, Kennedy turned to the pursuit of political power. He served in Franklin Roosevelt's administration as the first chairman of the Securities and Exchange Commission and as ambassador to the United Kingdom. When prohibition ended in 1933, Kennedy partnered with James Roosevelt (son of President Franklin Roosevelt) to found Somerset Importers to import Scotch Whiskey. While some Wall Street old guard might have looked down on Kennedy's religious and ethnic background, he still had an East Coast address.

While populists associated Wall Street with the eastern elite, Wall Street did not have a monopoly on financial dealings. Wells Fargo operated out of the west. Chicago businessmen Samuel Insull and Harold Stuart had enormous success in the utilities industry and formed a holding company, Insull Utilities Investments and International Securities Trust of America, hoping to challenge Wall Street's dominance. Mantis James Van Sweringen and Oris Paxton Van Sweringen, brothers from Ohio, developed the Shaker Heights community near Cleveland. From there they moved into interurban streetcars and railroads and then in to finance. The Van Sweringen brothers played a large role in the bubble of the late 1920s and became associated with J. P. Morgan and Company as the brothers became highly leveraged. In what would later be revealed as a typical story, they borrowed money to buy railroads, using those railroads as collateral to borrow more money to buy more railroads.

The Manipulators

Since some investors bet on rising stock values with borrowed money, it makes sense that they would manipulate stocks to ensure the desired result. We saw this with the persistent and aggressive boosterism found in the business press. Just as in politics, worry existed that voters would be manipulated. So, too, did the potential to manipulate the new democratically empowered investors, many of whom created pools to manipulate the market. A pool existed when a group of investors entered into an agreement to purchase a stock, often with the idea of increasing the value of that particular stock, but it could be a bear pool, too. Individuals in the pool would contribute money and hire a pool manager. The pool manager would then manipulate the stocks. A pool depended on the investing public buying into the rising prices. A good pool manager would create a high volume of activity with the stock, buying and selling stocks so that people following on the ticker tape would take note. The pool manager would reinforce this by planting stories with journalists who covered business. A. Newton Plummer, a public relations man, planted rumors with financial writers. Michael Meehan, a famous pool manager, began his career as a ticket broker on Broadway before moving on to the Curb Exchange and the New York Stock Exchange. Meehan made his name on Wall Street with the RCA pool. In 1928 Meehan attempted to corner the market on RCA stocks, making millions of dollars. After the 1929 stock market crash Meehan suffered from a breakdown and, eventually, was confined to a sanitarium.[4] He bribed journalist Richard Edmondson of the *Wall Street Journal* and W. F. Walmsley of the *New York Times* to boost stocks that his pool manipulated. The investing public then jumped on the bandwagon, pushing the stock prices higher. The pool manager had to time the sale of the pool's stock to maximize profit, a process that left the average investor holding a stock that had just crashed. Pools, in effect, created speculative bubbles with the idea that insiders would know when to sell, leaving outsiders to be the greater fools. During the 1920s corporate leaders joined pools involving their companies, sometimes belonging to a pool that short sold the company they ran.

Pools did not have to inflate stocks. The normal operation of the stock market saw ups and downs, bears and bulls. Early in the 1920s bear raids took place. Bears raiding Stutz Motors ran into problems when Allan A. Ryan, a prominent bull, cornered the market on Stutz Motors. He successfully squeezed the short sellers, forcing them to buy Stutz stock at very high prices. However, many of the men in the bear pool sat on the board of the Stock Exchange, which, in retaliation, forced Ryan out of the Stock Exchange and into bankruptcy. Ryan's failure to corner the market resulted in him owing over $32 million to such prominent backers as Charles Swab and Pierre DuPont.[5]

Famously, bears raided Clarence Saunders's Piggly Wiggly company in 1923. Saunders had begun as a clerk bagging groceries and rose to be the head of the grocery store chain. He unsuccessfully attempted to corner Piggly Wiggly stock to counter a bear raid. Saunders promised investors, who had lent him money against stock as collateral that they would "get it back from the market." However, the bear raiders forced the price of the stock down, and Saunders lost everything, including his company and his home, and he went $5 million in debt.[6]

Short sellers organized bear raids by taking a large position and then driving down the price of the stock by spreading rumors and other forms of manipulation. However, a bear raid is different from a bear, in that a bear believes that conditions are right for the stock to decline, while a bear raider tries to create a downward trajectory. Bear raids could be countered by cornering the stock, which means buying the outstanding shares of a stock, thus driving the price up.

The end result of the various manipulations of the stock market was that the public became both fascinated and cynical about the market. The rumor of the involvement of a famed pool manager could prompt the public into buying or selling. However, by the middle of the decade the Bull Market had driven out the bears.

The notion of easy money accompanied by high drama lured people to the stock market. Additionally, companies issued many of the hot stocks of the day. While managers and raiders clearly manipulated the markets, New Era companies made the products that promised to create the future. For example, RCA issued one of the hot stocks on the exchange. Commercial radio began in 1920 and promised to transform life. Joseph Kennedy's work with RKO had a similar dynamic. A person could buy a share of Hollywood glamour. Of course, Americans loved cars, so they demanded shares in General Motors. Although it was declining as a manufacturer, Studebaker—its cars often pictured full of college students—could still be the subject of one of the great stock market fights of the decade.

Brokerage firms also benefited from the entrance of new investors, one obvious point being that more investors meant more fees. Firms developed selling groups to service the general public. Brokerage firms also developed new ways, such as trusts, for the average person to invest. By 1927, firms had a two-tiered system of customers, with a preferred list and the general public. By the late 1920s even the staid companies, such as J. P. Morgan and Kuhn, Loeb, and Company, participated in preferred lists and risky ventures. Firms began establishing branch offices to cater to the investing public, a development that created a shortage of talent in the financial industry.

The Regulators

Although we have placed people into various categories, in reality these categories are more for our benefit. Toward the end of the decade, some in positions of responsibility identified speculation as a problem but identified few actual speculators. During the prosperity of the decade, the already difficult job of telling the speculator from the investor became even harder, out of the desire to keep the good times going. Policy makers and leaders rarely discussed curtailing speculation but instead focused on keeping the prosperity going. We see this when the economy slowed down. The 1920s economy, as good as it was, did have its ups and downs. In 1927 the economy slowed, so the Federal Reserve Board lowered the interest rates from 4 percent to 3.5 percent. The Federal Reserve followed this by purchasing securities on the open market to increase the money supply. Benjamin Strong, head of the New York Federal Reserve Bank, had another motivation for wanting to lower interest rates. Federal Reserve members also wanted to help the British and support the gold standard. The British could not maintain their gold reserves. They hoped that by lowering interest rates some of the surplus gold in the United States would return to Europe, which did not happen. British efforts to stay on the gold standard meant cheap money for the US financial system, fueling speculation.

The lower interest rates only made call money cheaper and speculation more attractive. The lowering of interest rates is controversial, because some economists and Federal Reserve officials feared Americans financed too many stock purchases with borrowed money. In January 1928, President Calvin Coolidge undercut any move to slow borrowing by publicly stating that brokerage loans were not too high. In an unprecedented move, the president had essentially endorsed more borrowing. At this time, presidents did not comment on the stock market and especially did not comment on the specifics of the market. However, it appeared that despite the slowing economy the Coolidge Prosperity would continue even as Coolidge announced he would not seek another term.

Given the fear of an economic slowdown, why did the stock market take off? The most basic answer is the easy money; also the public and investors both expected the economy to have ups and downs. Throughout the twenties the economy faltered slightly but then rallied to new heights. The slumps and rallies encouraged wealthy speculators, like W. C. Durant, to enter the market as they attempted to corner markets and drive up prices. Short sellers reentered the market, anticipating a slowing economy. However, short sellers remained vulnerable to corners. Bottom line, speculators counted on the mania of the crowds. In the spring of 1928 speculation began with stocks in General Motors, with American Telegraph and Telephone and General Electric following. Before long, RCA passed General Motors as the most valuable stock. The speculation spread to other stocks, including the retailer Montgomery Ward and aviation stocks. The ticker tape fell behind several times, and the stock market closed to give traders a chance to catch up with orders.

To counter the emerging speculative bubble, the Federal Reserve raised interest rates to 4 percent. This did not slow the market, so the Federal Reserve began to sell government bonds and, in May, raised interest rates again. In

May and June 1928, the stock market slowed and seemed as though it might become a bear market. However, another rally began on June 13 and 14, as speculators happily borrowed at the higher rate to buy stocks that seemed to promise even greater returns.

Not coincidentally, the markets rallied when the Republicans nominated Herbert Hoover on June 14. Hoover, in his acceptance speech, promised the end of the poorhouse. Bankers and the public expected Hoover would be even better for the markets than Coolidge. While Hoover would win an easy victory, investors had little to fear, whichever way the election went. The Democrats nominated Alfred Smith of New York, a Catholic with ties to Tammany Hall. Smith, no foe of Wall Street, installed John J. Raskob, of DuPont and General Motors, as chairman of the Democratic National Committee. Raskob vocally boosted the New Era prosperity. He would go on to argue in *Ladies' Home Journal* that everyone should be rich.[7] Raskob moved the Democratic National Committee headquarters to the General Motors building in New York City.

In November 1928 the nation elected Herbert Hoover president and experienced the Hoover Bull Market. On November 23, the Stock Exchange reached 7 million shares traded. RCA, Montgomery Ward, and Packard hit highs that had been previously unthinkable. Investors and brokers abandoned the old rule of thumb that a stock should be worth ten times its earnings. The market slumped slightly in December, but a speculative market emerged.

The newly elected President Hoover, ever the efficiency expert, acted quickly to convene conferences to address the nation's problems. The report of the Committee on Recent Economic Changes of the President's Conference on Unemployment embodied Hoover's faith in progressive engineering. The committee noted that each generation tends to view its economic situation as new and unique. However, the committee argued that "the changes have not been in structure but in speed and spread." With the stock market, the committee estimated that the number of people who owned shares had grown from 2 million to more than 17 million. These new investors, many of whom were speculators, invested their savings but also had borrowed enough to strain the credit structure of the country. It concluded that "the consequences of this process cannot be measured at this time."[8]

Hoover's report seemed to fly in the face of business as usual. In September 1929, just seven weeks before the stock market crash, McGraw-Hill launched a new magazine, *The Business Week* (later to become *Businessweek*) to compete with *Forbes* magazine. The editors of *The Business Week* adopted the new magazine format and focused on the domestic economy. However, rather than ride the wave of New Era prosperity, the magazine's first decade saw the Great Depression.

The Boosters

The hubris of the 1920s stock market is hard to miss. Several people are destined to be remembered for foolishly proclaiming their faith in New Era prosperity only to see the arrival of the Great Depression. Economist Irving Fisher, a pioneer in his field and a New Era booster, almost destroyed his reputation by declaring right before the crash that "stock prices have reached what looks like a permanently high plateau." This ranks close to Herbert Hoover's 1928 prediction that poverty would end in America. It would be easy to compile a long list of prominent politicians and financiers all proclaiming the soundness of the markets in 1928 and 1929. While it is understandable why bankers, making large sums of money, would boost the market, especially when many of them were also highly leveraged, it is not so easy to understand the near universality of the booster spirit. Although they were subsequently vilified, Fisher and Hoover were smart, admired men. Fisher invested heavily in the market and would lose everything in the crash. Hoover's political fortune also rose and fell with the market. In 1932 he would lose reelection dramatically and decisively. Why didn't anyone see the bubble? How could so many smart men have been so foolish? The answers are the same as with all other bubbles. They were making too much money. Those who predicted a crash were dismissed. Political leaders did not want to say the unpopular thing. It did seem that this time everything was different.

By the middle of the decade, the stock market had achieved a cult status that made it difficult to criticize. Although Alexander Noyes warned of market corrections in the pages of the *New York Times,* people did not listen, despite his standing as a respected longtime observer of the stock market. From 1891 to 1920 Noyes had worked as the financial editor of the *New York Evening Post,* and in 1920 he assumed the financial editorship of the *Times.* Noyes did not buy the New Era theory that the markets would not crash again. While he later said that he received unhappy letters from readers when he predicted that the Bull Market would not last, his obituary carried the headline, "Financial Editor since 1920 Warned Public of Coming Crash Long before 1929." In congressional testimony, Noyes said that his lack of faith in the New Era and his predictions had made him "the most unpopular man in the community."[9] While Noyes gained redemption during the 1930s for his advocacy of the long view and sound money, during the twenties he swam against the tide. Noyes would go down in history as a highly respected financial journalist, in part because he resisted the cult of the market and in part because, unlike other financial journalists at the time, he did not take money to promote stocks.

The media often promoted the New Era economy rather than asking tough questions. More often than should have been the case, business writers saw their jobs as promoting the virtues of the stock market, not critical reporting. The tone of business reporting tended to follow Warren G. Harding's advice from his days as a newspaper publisher and editor: "boost, don't knock." A prime example of this was *Barron's National Financial Weekly* (later just *Barron's*) founded in 1921 by Clarence W. Barron. As president of Dow Jones & Company, he also controlled the *Wall Street Journal,* so *Barron's* complemented the newspaper, and both took bullish positions. All of this made Barron a power in financial circles. His obituary, admittedly from the *New York Times,* noted that he "gained the friendship and confidence of many of the leaders of speculative finance at a time when Wall Street contained some of its most picturesque figures." Politically, he supported the Republican ascendency. He staunchly opposed Woodrow Wilson.[10] In 1932 congressional investigations into the stock market crash revealed that reporters for the *Wall Street Journal* had accepted bribes to promote stocks.

John J. Raskob is another man whose boosterism knew few limits and, ultimately, seemed ill timed. Raskob worked as the treasurer for DuPont. When DuPont purchased General Motors, Raskob became the vice president for finance for both companies. At General Motors, Raskob created the General Motors Acceptance Corporation, which allowed GM to directly finance car purchases. From there, Raskob entered into the public limelight. It is worth noting that Raskob sold his stocks in General Motors to build the Empire State Building. From 1928 to 1932 he served as chairman of the Democratic National Committee, strongly supporting New York governor Alfred E. Smith's losing 1928 presidential campaign. After Franklin Roosevelt's election, he stepped down from the Democratic Party position. Raskob and Smith would play key roles in the American Liberty League, which opposed Roosevelt in the 1936 election.

Raskob's status as a public figure lent weight to his words when Samuel Crowther interviewed him for an article entitled "Everybody Ought to Be

Rich," which appeared in 1929 just before the stock market crashed. It is indicative that this was the peak of the cult of the stock market that the article appeared in *Ladies' Home Journal,* a magazine not normally noted for its financial coverage. Raskob argued that the stock market made it possible to become rich by investing $15 a month. Raskob's cavalier attitude toward attaining wealth also underscored the raised expectations of the new consumerism and the gap between the rich and everyone else. He defined what it meant to be rich: "Being rich is, of course, a comparative status. A man with a million dollars used to be considered rich, but so many people have at least that much these days, or are earning incomes in excess of a normal return from a million dollars, that a millionaire does not cause any comment." While it would be easy enough to find people who were not so cavalier about having a million dollars, Raskob defined wealth in terms of living from investments rather than from wages. A man achieved wealth when he could comfortably support his family from investments, a status that, he argued, was within everyone's grasp, thanks to the booming stock market. Of course, he acknowledged, the economy would contain inequalities, but he explained that inequality resulted from an individual's poor investment strategies. "It is quite true that wealth is not so evenly distributed as it ought to be and as it can be. And part of the reason for the unequal distribution is the lack of systematic investment and also the lack of even moderately sensible investment." His approach to investing reflected the consumer culture of the decade. Those investors who did not become wealthy fell into three categories. The first put their money into savings banks that paid fixed interest rates. A second tried to get rich quick, buying a "wildcat security." The third did not save at all, believing that fixed rates were not enough and did not want to risk being defrauded. "It may be said that this is a phenomenal increase and that conditions are going to be different in the next ten years. That prophecy may be true, but it is not founded on experience. In my opinion the wealth of the country is bound to increase at a very rapid rate."[11]

Raskob made all the classic New Era arguments. He went so far as to proclaim, "We have scarcely started." The Bull Market made investing a practical way for everyone to achieve comfort. He claimed that "the obstacles to being rich are two: The trouble of saving, and the trouble for finding a medium for investment." If one could overcome these, one could join the comfortably wealthy. The market, according to him, had its own psychology that ensured prosperity. One did not have to worry about declining stocks or companies going under. He wrote, "Prosperity is in the nature of an endless chain, and we can break it only by our own refusal to see what it is." The investor provides companies with capital; in turn the investor can consume more based on the return on the investment. For those who still viewed stocks as a dubious place to put their money, he assured them that stocks are just as safe as bonds or mortgages, because "there are very few failures among the larger corporations."[12] His argument that modern corporations were too big to fail should sound familiar. In the unlikely event of a failure, the company will go through bankruptcy and be bought, thus protecting investors. The ability to borrow fueled the new prosperity, the same borrowing power that had brought about the consumer revolution.

Raskob found the old maxims about thrift just as wrong as socialism. He argued that "most of the old precepts contrasting the immorality of speculation with the morality of sound investment have no basis in fact. They have just been so often repeated as true that they are taken as true." Borrowing to buy stocks is a method of earning. A person should not fear the stock market. It is not gambling, because "the line between investment and speculation is a very hazy one, and a definition is not to be found in the legal form of a security or in limiting the possible return on the money. The difference is rather in the approach."[13] Success depended on buying quality stocks as investments. According to him, many people predicted that buying a car on installments would lead to ruin, but instead new industries arose around the industry. For Raskob and other disciples of the market, the new consumerism combined with the Bull Market to produce an endless bounty of wealth. Raskob went beyond Herbert Hoover. Hoover predicted the end of the poorhouse, while Raskob seemingly pointed to a future where everyone who wanted to could live off his or her investments. All Americans had to do was have faith in the new tools of consumerism and in the stock market.

With boosters such as Mitchell and Raskob urging the average American to get into the stock market, what did the stock market look like to such a person? How would he or she invest? The Bull Market went hand in hand with changes in how companies financed their operations and the growing public familiarity with the markets. The 1920s saw a fundamental shift in how people viewed money, particularly debt. Raskob certainly emphasized this with both his work at General Motors and his boosting of the stock market. The average person became more comfortable with buying through borrowing, and also with the idea of owning debt.

4 How the Economy Crashed

How Did the Great Depression Begin?

HISTORIANS, ECONOMISTS, AND POLITICIANS vigorously debate the link between the stock market crash of 1929 and the Great Depression. In the simplest of terms the contrast between the 1920s and the 1930s could not be better for debating the nature of the economy and the role of the government in it. Under close examination the simple dichotomy between the small government of the 1920s and the big government of the 1930s gives way to a more complex story. The bursting stock market bubble also burst the idea that the stock market created a commonwealth of shared prosperity, a Jeffersonian end produced with Hamiltonian tools. The ambiguity helps feed an ongoing ideological and political debate over the role of the government in the markets and the nature of markets. The difficulty lies in establishing precise causation, especially when focusing on a single variable in a highly complex system such as the stock market or the US economy. The people operating, and operating in, this complex system were guided by expectations based on the past as well as the fear of losing everything. For our purposes of explaining how the stock market crashed, we are setting aside, to the extent possible, the ideological debate to look at how the crash did or did not fit into patterns of other bubbles bursting. We'll then lay out some of the economic issues surrounding the crash and the start of the Great Depression.

The Depression that followed the stock market crash is what makes the crash historically significant and politically contentious. There have been market crashes that did not result in a general economic collapse. If the years following 1929 had seen a mild recession, we would not care much about October 1929. Its context imbues the 1929 crash with importance. A great deal of the writing on the crash is an attempt to access the role of institutions such as the Federal Reserve or New Deal agencies. Whether or not the crash directly caused the Depression, in 1929 Americans blamed the crash, regarding it as a serious blow to the economy. Americans acted accordingly, if not always wisely.

When considering the linkage between the crash and the Depression, the old cliché of a perfect storm fits. A key point that sometimes gets lost in the debate over what caused the Depression is that, rather than a single event, there took place a series of interconnected events that lapped over the nation's economy like waves. While this might seem obvious, imagine living through the period from 1929 to 1933. On top of the stock market crash, the list of additional economic problems and emergencies is daunting. It includes rising consumer debt, falling agricultural prices resulting in a farming crisis, German reparation payments as well as British and French war debt threatening European stability, Latin American debt defaults, three nationwide waves of bank failures, and the collapse of the gold standard. Any one of these would be a significant challenge, but when put together, you get the Great Depression.

What Caused the Crash?

The short answer is that we are not sure what caused the bubble to burst. The standard explanation is that speculators had driven the price of stocks too high, but accounts usually describe the process of panic selling, not the reason why the panic selling started. Before discussing the specifics of the 1929 stock market crash, it is worth reviewing some items. The bubble preceded the crash. While it is true that October 1929 burst the New Era psychology of the 1920s, it is not entirely clear what triggered it. Some crashes have a specific trigger, but not so in 1929. A mania sustained the downward trajectory of prices once it started. Some economists have dug into the stock market, looking specifically at instability in the utilities and trusts (which were similar to modern mutual funds and invested heavily in utilities) as the event that triggered the crash. These large, interlocking financial structures were an unstable house of cards. Others argue that the crash started in Europe and spread to America. Hoover favored this explanation. One school of thought argues that the overinflation of the money supply during the twenties created the Depression. The October crash painfully corrected to the overinvestment of the previous decade. All of these can be added to the list of economic problems that fed into the Great Depression.

Hubris blinded investors, the faith that this time the prosperity would go on forever. While many things played into this hubris, the belief that the Federal Reserve System would prevent another panic played an important role in the bubble and the crash. Benjamin Strong, chairman of the Federal Reserve Bank of New York and a close ally to Wall Street and the Bank of London, reinforced this idea. He said that "the Federal Reserve System is a safeguard against anything like a calamity growing out of money rates. Not only have we the power to deal with such an emergency instantly by flooding the Street with money, but I think the country is well aware of this and probably places reliance upon the common sense and power of the system. In former days the psychology was different because the facts of the banking situation were different. Mob panic, and consequently mob disaster, is less likely to arise."[1] The short-lived recession of 1920–21 and the economic dips during the decade reinforced this view. Policy makers and journalists promoted the belief that the actions of the Federal Reserve and the Harding administration had effectively combated the economic downturn. The recoveries that followed the dips in the market supported this idea. The magic formula for ongoing prosperity had been found.

Certainly in October 1929 investors panicked, but the fear went beyond Wall Street into the broader economy. Just as New Era boosterism contained an element of self-fulfillment, so too did the panic that followed October 1929. The stock market had been promoted as a perpetual motion machine of prosperity, and it had failed. As the market crashed, political and financial leaders failed to act. Many of the young men working on Wall Street during the boom times did not remember the Panic of 1907. They deluded themselves into thinking it could not happen again or if it did the Fed would fix it quickly.

The Psychology of the Speculative Market

Again, it is difficult to put a precise date on when the Bull Market turned into a speculative market. As John Raskob pointed out, there is a gray area in defining speculation. The market always has speculative and conservative investors; it is more a question of balance than of absolutes. Another factor with rampant speculation is that aspects of the market that are benign or beneficial during normal times become exaggerated, or even dangerous. As John Kenneth Galbraith explains, "One of the paradoxes of speculation in securities is that the loans that underwrite it are among the safest of all investments. They are protected by stocks which under ordinary circumstances are instantly salable and by cash margin as well. The money, as noted, can be retrieved on demand."[2] One economist dates early 1928 as the time when the "true speculative orgy, started in earnest."[3] Early 1928 saw a high rise in margin buying as increasing numbers of people purchased stocks with increasingly expensive call loans. Speculators had no interest in dividends, but rather in watching the stock increase in value so they could sell it.

Especially during the 1920s, market watchers commonly reported, and seemingly believed, that a small group of influential businessmen who could guarantee ongoing prosperity and bull markets manipulated the markets. Therefore, the public, especially the investing public, paid close attention to the pronouncements of top investors, businessmen, and political leaders. The public assumed they had inside knowledge and manipulated the market through pools and other mechanisms. Rather than condemning the manipulation, in the 1920s boosters argued that everyone could get rich by being on the right side of the manipulation. The rich might see the greatest benefit, but others could also see gains. Somewhat famously John Raskob commented that General Motors should sell at twelve times earnings (ten is the standard). Soon, GM stocks soared. Academic economists joined in cheering on the Bull Market. Yale's Irving Fisher praised the businessmen who ran the market for "their vision for the future and boundless hope and optimism." Before leaving office, in his 1928 State of the Union Address, Calvin Coolidge said, "No Congress of the United States has met with a more pleasing prospect than that which appears at the present time. In the domestic field there is tranquility and contentment . . . and the highest record of years of prosperity." The source of this prosperity, he concluded "lies in the integrity and character of the American people."[4]

A lot of people in leadership positions felt the need to wash their hands of the stock market bubble after the fact, an act of hindsight with 20/20 vision. Prior to the crash, no consensus existed as to what, if anything, ailed the markets. Some kept their doubts private. In accepting the nomination to follow Coolidge into the White House, Herbert Hoover continued this theme, foreseeing a future without the poorhouse. To be fair to Hoover, as secretary of commerce, he had warned President Coolidge about "the growing tide of speculation" as early as 1925.[5] Hoover, the engineer and planner, wanted more controls on finance, but the public, or Wall Street, did not know this. In fact, some New Era boosters warned of a business depression if Al Smith won, despite his close association with Raskob. The day after Hoover's victory, the markets boomed to new highs, in large part because investors believed that Hoover would continue Coolidge's policies.

Those who publicly predicted difficulties in the market before the crash were dismissed. Financier Paul M. Warburg, a founder of the Federal Reserve System, warned of disaster if "unrestrained speculation" in the stock market did not end. Boosters accused him of attempting to undermine American prosperity.[6] Alexander Noyes, the *New York Times* financial editor, saw trouble as well. The newspaper received letters of complaint from those who had missed out on part of the boom because they had followed Noyes's advice.

Structural Issues in the Market

Volatility characterized the stock market in the months leading up to the crash. In and of itself this did not spook investors, nor should it have; some argued it signaled that speculation might be abating. When the market rose, it did so in leaps and bounds. The industrial average rose 25 points in March 1928 alone. The stock market dipped in June and in December in 1928. On December 8, RCA fell 72 points. Despite these ups and downs, the market had a good year. The *Times* industrial average went from 245 to 331. RCA, the darling technology stock, went from 85 to 420. Montgomery Ward saw a remarkable rise from 117 to 440. Trading volume reached new highs; brokers traded 920,550,032 shares in 1928, compared to 576,990,875 in 1927. Likewise 1929 also saw dips, one in March and one in May. Stocks dipped again in September 1929 only to rally before finally bursting in October. The larger point is that a reasonable person might have expected a corrective bear market. However, as Frederick Lewis Allen wrote in *Only Yesterday,* by October 4 a "good many stocks had coasted to what seemed first-class bargain levels," so investors anticipating the rebound took the slumps as an opportunity to buy.[7]

Buying on margin fueled the speculative boom. According to the Federal Reserve Bank of New York, broker loans reached $6,804,000,000 in early October, as margin buyers continued to enter the market. People borrowed a lot of money to speculate in the stock market. A person buying a security on margin gained the value of ownership as if he or she had purchased it outright with cash. In other words, no penalty existed for partially owning a stock. During the 1920s margin rates hit the 45 percent to 50 percent range, but in some instances the stocks became collateral for further loans, meaning that speculators might have only a small stake in the collateral they put up. One would borrow money to buy stocks and then use those stocks as collateral to borrow more money; that money then bought more stocks. Furthermore, banks had established brokerage houses. A bank would loan money to a brokerage house. The broker then lent it to a margin buyer, who then bought stocks from the broker using those stocks as collateral to the banks.

That Americans used trusts to invest reinforced the cycle of borrowing and buying. An average person looking to make a few dollars probably did not individually purchase stocks. Instead, he or she bought into a trust. Trusts had operated in Europe for some time but started in the United States in 1921. Initially, trusts operated much like a modern mutual fund, with investors buying shares of the trust and the trust publishing an investment portfolio. Trusts often purchased specific securities, so while an investor did not pick stocks the investor understood the investment profile of the trust. However, by the late 1920s, given the nature of the market, trust operators did not want to indicate which stocks they purchased. Public information of a trust making large moves, buying or selling, could distort markets. In some instances, the trust morphed into a business that sold shares of it. Trust began to take advantage of leverage, the same thing that made buying on margin such a powerful tool. Just as an individual who invested $10 to purchase $100 worth of stock would realize a 100 percent gain when the stock reached $110, the same thing applied to a trust. Trusts, however, had one additional advantage. Trusts could multiply this by creating other trusts in a pyramid scheme. For example, an investment bank creates a trust company that then, borrowing money from the parent bank, invests on margin, thus utilizing leverage. If that original trust then creates a second, subsidiary, trust the subsidiary trust could take some of the leveraged assets of the first trust and use that to invest on margin a second time. This multiplied the power of leverage. Obviously, as long as prices increased a great deal of money could be made. Just as obviously, leverage could work in reverse if prices fell. Falling prices would mean disaster.

By the fall of 1929, bankers and investors had constructed the market on a foundation of money borrowed to leverage greater returns upon the belief in ever rising prices. So strongly did they believe in the market that even when it faltered investors jumped in, often with more borrowed money. Ironically, the ability to borrow and invest that in normal times served a positive purpose became part of an unstable and unsustainable market that eventually collapsed. Investors—speculators—in the market did not sell, for fear of missing out on a fortune. Surely, a greater fool would stay in the market just a bit longer. This psychological state could change easily. Bubbles burst; they always do. So in one sense the exact trigger isn't important. However, in the immediate aftermath of the bubble New Era boosters blamed the end of the ride on two incidents. They blamed it, first, on the failure of the Hatry Financial Group in England in September. As the second culprit, they identified the refusal of the Massachusetts Department of Public Utilities to allow Edison Electric to split its stocks.

Why Didn't the Government Stop the Bubble?

Did the probusiness and Wall Street–friendly political climate of the twenties contribute to the crash? Politicians, as we have seen, encouraged the building excitement about Wall Street. However, political leaders still operated in the wake of the Panic of 1907, the Progressive Era, and World War I. They had experienced panics and periods of economic planning. As secretary of commerce, Herbert Hoover had actively encouraged business cooperation and modernization. Congress mandated that the Federal Reserve Board try to prevent bubbles and act as a lender of last resort in the event of a crash. Board members, such as Strong, assured the public it would act. Ironically, the Great Engineer Hoover put off acting, in the belief that it was the Federal Reserve Board's responsibility to do so. Why then, did the Federal Reserve allow the bubble to continue?

John Kenneth Galbraith's answer was that the Federal Reserve failed to act because it was a "body of startling incompetence."[8] Warren G. Harding had appointed Daniel R. Crissinger as chairman of the Federal Reserve Board. Crissinger, a neighbor and friend of the president, had as his qualification that he had served as president of the Marion Steam Shovel Company but otherwise had no experience or expertise in banking or economics. In 1927 Roy Young replaced Crissinger. Young, a career banker who served as head of two Federal Reserve Banks, served through the crisis of 1929 and resigned as chairman in August 1930. Young attempted to address speculation by championing the policy of pressuring banks to stop lending for speculation rather than raising the interest rates. During the buildup and crisis, the Federal Reserve Board seemed most interested in avoiding responsibility.

During this period with a weak Reserve Board, leadership came from the New York Federal Reserve Bank under Benjamin Strong. Strong had made the New York Federal Reserve Bank the dominant voice in the Federal Reserve System. He advocated for solid money and acted as an ally of Britain. Strong cooperated with J. P. Morgan and Company, another bastion of Anglophiles, to aid the Bank of England in restoring the gold standard. To slow the flow of gold into the United States, which had a large surplus after the war, he eased American money rates, making the United States a less attractive place to store gold. Not everyone agreed with Strong. Lower interest rates had contributed to the easy money that fueled Wall Street speculation. Even an internationalist like Hoover called Strong a "mental annex to Europe."[9]

However, Strong, who suffered from tuberculosis, died in October 1928. George L. Harrison succeeded him. Strong's death created a power struggle within the Federal Reserve System, and the Federal Reserve Board began to exert more influence. The transition helps explain some significant mistakes and inconsistencies in Federal Reserve policy.

To be fair, the Federal Reserve faced large problems. It is difficult to slow a bubble gently without bursting it. The Federal Reserve had two primary tools. The Federal Reserve could raise the rediscount rate, making money more expensive but, as we have seen, this would make the United States an even more attractive haven for gold. In February 1929 the New York Federal Reserve Bank advocated raising the interest rate to 6 percent. The Federal Reserve Board declined to do so, preferring "moral suasion" to direct action. That February the Bank of England announced a rate hike, from 4.5 percent to 5.5 percent, in an attempt to slow the flow of gold from England into the United States. The rate hike had minimal impact on the markets. Given the returns on the stock market, the interest rates would have had to be significantly higher to slow the bubble, high enough to damage the rest of the economy.

For its second tool, the Federal Reserve could sell government securities on the open market to draw cash out of the economy, thus sterilizing the money. Money kept in the Federal Reserve's vaults could not fuel speculation. This policy did not work; the Federal Reserve did not have enough securities to sell because of the lack of government debt. At the beginning of 1928 the Federal Reserve had $617 million and sold heavily during the first half of the year in an attempt to reduce the money supply. By the end of the year it had $228 million. Although these seem like large numbers, the Fed did not have enough to dry up the money supply flowing through Wall Street.

Furthermore, banks that were not under the purview of the Federal Reserve System loaned money for speculation. In early 1929 call loans carried an interest rate of 5 percent. By the end of the year, that reached 12 percent. As previously mentioned, the high interest rates created a flood of gold into the United States, thus increasing the money supply. Beyond this, American corporations found it attractive to make their cash available on the call loan market. Standard Oil of New Jersey contributed $69 million to the call market. The Federal Reserve System lacked the power to influence this money supply. For manufacturers, it would be difficult to realize a 12 percent return by selling products. Banks would happily borrow money from the Federal Reserve at the rate of 5 or 6 percent and lend it out as call loans at 12 percent. By early 1929 banks contributed only about half of the money available for call loans.

With the death of Benjamin Strong, Adolph Miller became the new intellectual force at the Federal Reserve Board. An academic economist whose appointment to the board dated back to 1914, Miller argued for the Real Bills Doctrine, which was generally accepted by economists and bankers. It had been a guiding idea in the creation of the Federal Reserve System. According to the doctrine, if new money entered the economy in support of production (i.e., people used it to build things) then the money would not create inflation. When a bank creates debt it also increases the money supply, which has the potential to create price inflation. The doctrine holds that if that debt is backed by something real (i.e., something is produced with the money), then it will not create price inflation. The Real Bills Doctrine went hand in hand with the gold standard, in that it created, in theory, a stable self-regulating currency. Under the doctrine money loaned for intangible purposes (e.g., speculating on the stock market) would be inflationary. Miller, following this doctrine, pressured member banks to loan money only for nonspeculative reasons. The difficulty lay in identifying speculators among those borrowing money.

At the end of March the Federal Reserve Board began meeting daily to discuss the issue of speculation. Although the board issued no statements, Wall Street feared that the Federal Reserve might take more aggressive action to slow the stock market. Prices began to decline, and brokers asked for more margin. Stoked by fears of Federal Reserve action, the interest rate on call money spiked. At this moment Charles E. Mitchell stepped in. Mitchell's jobs had included president of National City Bank, one of the largest in the country, and director of the New York Federal Reserve Bank. He informed the press that "we feel that we have an obligation which is paramount to any Federal Reserve warning, or anything else, to avert any dangerous crisis in the money market."[10] National City Bank would make money available, borrowing it from the New York Federal Reserve Bank if necessary. In August the Federal Reserve Board raised interest rates to 6 percent. The markets rallied. Following this the Federal Reserve Board "retired from the field."[11] President Hoover then attempted to slow speculation through persuasion, dispatching an emissary to Wall Street. He then summoned Richard Whitney of the New York Stock Exchange to the White House to discuss speculation, but he did nothing. The Dow Jones Industrial Average peaked at 381.2 in September 1929.

Black Thursday

The September peak lasted a long time. During the early parts of October, the stock market jumped around, declining on October 3, 4, and 16 and creating some concern. In mid-October Charles Mitchell reassured investors: "Although in some cases speculation has gone too far in the United States, the markets generally are now in a healthy condition. The last six weeks have done an immense amount of good by shaking down prices. . . . The market values have a sound basis in the general prosperity of our country." At this moment economist and New Era champion Irving Fisher nearly ruined his reputation with predictions of a new, permanent plateau in the stock market. There had been previous downturns in the Bull Market, and it did not seem unreasonable to expect another upturn.

The first signs of the stock market crash appeared on Wednesday, October 23, when the markets saw a massive sell-off of over 6 million shares. When the stock market reopened on Thursday, October 24, stock prices remained steady for the first hour but then fell sharply on heavy trading. As prices fell, investors who had bought on margin were forced to sell, as leverage worked against them. Banks, having accepted stocks as collateral for call loans, watched the value of those assets fall. Brokers called for increased margins. Speculators had to increase the amount of money they had committed to the ownership of the stock. Those who could not do so were forced to sell. Banks faced the reality that the collateral on their call loans, with each passing moment, lost value or, as the crash continued, became worthless. With prices falling and collateral values declining, the banks faced a liquidity crisis and called in the loans. Remember, call loans were made on a day-to-day basis. In good times, banks could let the loans ride, but now they were calling them in, forcing more selling.

The "blue chip" stocks of the Bull Market, including those New Era stocks that were never supposed to drop, declined. US Steel fell from 205½ to 193½; GE fell from 400 to 283; RCA from 68¾ to 44½. The market fell 33 points, or 9 percent, in a single day. The Dow Jones Industrial Average fell to 299, a 21 percent decline from the peak. Selling reached such a volume that the ticker tape feed fell behind, leaving investors with no way of following markets. In the confusion speculators blindly sold out of fear.

At this point financial leaders revisited their actions of the 1907 Bankers' Panic. In 1907 the senior J. P. Morgan had led the effort to stop the panic. By 1929 his son and namesake enjoyed a life of semiretirement that included travel and art collecting. Still, the markets looked to J. P. Morgan and Company for help. When journalists noticed that Charles Mitchell had slipped into 23 Wall Street, talk began to circulate of "organized support," meaning a bankers' pool to stop the crash. With J. P. Morgan in Europe, it fell to Thomas Lamont, the senior partner at J. P. Morgan and Company, to organize a rescue effort. Lamont, a highly influential partner at the firm, stood as the quintessential banker and diplomat of the decade. Meeting with Lamont and Mitchell were a who's who of banking that included Albert H. Wiggin of Chase National Bank, William Potter of Guaranty Trust Company, Seward Prosser of Bankers Trust Company, and George F. Baker Jr. of First National Bank. Each man agreed to contribute $40 million to a $240 million pool to shore up the stock market. They needed to reverse the psychology of the panic. It is worth remembering at this point that while the bankers organized their pool the Federal Reserve had a mandate to act as lender of last resort to stop panics.

As the pool formed, Lamont met with reporters in an effort to reassure the public. He gave one of the great understatements in history: "There has been a little distress selling on the Stock Exchange and we have held a meeting of the heads of several financial institutions to discuss the situation. We have found that there are no houses in difficulty and reports from brokers indicate that margins are being maintained satisfactorily." This is when Richard Whitney, vice president of the New York Stock Exchange and brother of Morgan partner George Whitney, appeared on the floor as the pool's agent. He dramatically bid a high $205 for 10,000 shares of US Steel. He then proceeded to purchase stocks throughout the market. As noted earlier, Whitney symbolically purchased US Steel, which was significant because of its status as one of the largest corporations in the United States. It was also symbolically important as a creation of J. P. Morgan.

Prior to the 1930s the New York Stock Exchange functioned more as a club than a corporation, the quintessential good old boys' network of gentleman bankers, a club Whitney belonged to. Brokers knew he spoke for J. P. Morgan and Company and similar old banking firms. With news of a bankers' pool, prices stabilized and even rallied a bit. Still, over 12 million shares changed hands. The ticker tape and clerks were woefully behind, leaving financiers and investors in the dark. Rumors circulated that speculators were committing suicide and that the Chicago exchange had closed. President Hoover reassured the public that "the fundamental business of the country, that is, production and distribution of commodities, is on a sound and prosperous basis." Then prices readily dropped below Whitney's bid; the bankers' pool failed. The bankers now changed tactics. Rather than boosting the market, they attempted to plug the "air holes," which occurred when people offered stock for sale with no buyer in sight. That Monday, stocks lost about 13 percent of their value.

On Black Tuesday, October 29, the markets again fell into panic, as investors started dumping stocks, often into air holes with no buyers. Call loans were secured by now-worthless stocks. This created a crisis for the banks. If the banks called in the loans and the debtors could not pay, it would do the banks no good to seize worthless collateral. As this dynamic drove prices lower, a second rescue effort appeared. William Durant—formerly of General Motors and now a stock speculator—and the Rockefeller family began pumping money into the stock market in an attempt to halt the slide. The Rockefellers, in particular, made a point of reassuring the public that they bought solid, conservative stocks as a hedge against the panic. Still, stocks fell another 12 percent. Wednesday, October 30, saw a rally, but trading volume had been enormous, as had been the losses. Whitney announced that the market would close for half a day on Thursday and all day Friday and Saturday.

More than a few people were surprised by the intensity of the stock market crash. At its end, stocks lost 90 percent of their value. By November the market reached 199 and lost $30 billion. Prominent economists John Maynard Keynes and Irving Fisher both lost money in the crash. Fisher lost all of his wealth, including his house. Keynes had made a fortune in the markets, lost most of it in the crash, and later rebuilt it.

Even as the stock market crashed, boosters downplayed its importance. David Dubinsky, president of the International Ladies' Garment Workers' Union predicted that the stock market crash would be good for the textile industry. He theorized that the crash would make industrial leaders focus on sober production and not risky financial speculation.[12] Another article predicted that the crash would free funds for the rest of the economy.[13]

The Response

While Wall Street understood that Whitney represented "organized support" from the "big boys" of Wall Street, there remained the question why the Federal Reserve did not act as Congress and the public expected. Strong had promised that the New York Federal Reserve would flood the market with money in the event of a panic. However, the Federal Reserve Board remained silent as the bankers' pool attempted to stop the panic.

The inaction of the Federal Reserve Board is a black mark on its history that remains controversial. Monetarist economists call the Great Depression the Great Contraction, because the board allowed the money supply to contract by about one-third following the crash. The crash did not cause the Depression, but the subsequent shrinking of the money supply that contributed to massive bank failures did. When the Federal Reserve allowed banks to collapse rather than acting as a lender of last resort, it facilitated a panic in the banking system that resulted in bank runs. This inaction combined with the board's lack of action in dealing with the liquidity crisis following the crash turned what would have been an ordinary recession into a depression. In its defense the Federal Reserve felt constrained by the requirement, imposed by the Federal Reserve Act, that Federal Reserve notes be backed by gold. Policies devised to preserve sound money and to prevent an inflated currency backfired in a deflationary period.

With the Federal Reserve Board and the bankers' pool failing to stymie the panic, it fell to Congress and the president to act. Hoover began with public reassurances. A panic is a psychological event. The bankers understood this.

It's worth remembering that the Great Depression had not started during the October crash. There were troubling signs in the economy, but hardly on the scale of what would follow. The initial financial crisis can be measured in months. During this time, Hoover called in business leaders for a series of meetings and conferences that resulted in public pledges not to cut wages, production, and prices. As the Depression emerged, Hoover hoped to deal with the economic meltdown through volunteerism. Not surprisingly, Hoover's initial response looked like his work at the Department of Commerce or a voluntary version of the War Industries Board of World War I.

Meanwhile, the Smoot-Hawley Tariff (officially the Tariff Act of 1930) worked its way through Congress. The Smoot-Hawley Tariff has assumed a reputation as one of the great blunders in American economic history, but at the time it seemed an orthodox move. Talk of raising tariffs predated the crash. Sponsored by Republican senator Reed Smoot and representative Willis Hawley, the legislation put into place a high protective tariff. Although they now consider the tariff a mistake, at the time Republicans were the party of protective tariffs. During the nineteenth century Republicans raised the tariff with the promise that it would protect both jobs and businesses. As the primary sponsor of the legislation, William McKinley rode the "McKinley Tariff" to the White House. In 1922 Republicans raised the tariff after Wilson and Democrats had cut it. As a presidential candidate, Hoover promised farmers he would increase the tariff on agricultural goods to aid the farm crisis. Following the election both houses of Congress began working on higher tariffs, particularly with an eye toward protecting agriculture.

However, protective tariffs did not sit well with politicians and businesses with international connections. In May 1930, over 1,000 economists, including Irving Fisher, signed a petition opposing the tariff. Henry Ford opposed the legislation. Thomas Lamont, of J. P. Morgan and Company, almost begged Hoover not to sign it. The tariff passed with overwhelming Republican support, putting Hoover in a position where he felt he had to sign it, after his campaign pledges. The tariff debate highlights the tensions that existed between international bankers like J. P. Morgan and Republicans, particularly those from the Midwest and the West, where protectionism remained popular and bankers were not. Morgan partners liked Republican sound money, low taxes, and small government domestic policies but disliked isolationism. With the Smoot-Hawley Tariff the United States led the world into an age of economic nationalism.

Senator Reed Smoot and Representative Willis Hawley after passage of the tariff that bears their name. The Smoot-Hawley Tariff is often considered a reason for the worsening Depression, and to this day, it is cited as an example of bad economic policy. *Source:* National Photo Company, via Wikimedia Commons (public domain).

Initially, it appeared as though Congress and the president had met with success. The first three months of 1930 saw a "Little Bull Market," to use Frederick Lewis Allen's phrase. Keynes and Fisher both believed the crisis had ended by April 1930, as the stock market experienced something of a rally. Manufacturing increased, seemingly validating the protectionism of the new, record-high tariffs. However, Smoot-Hawley sparked retaliation by trading partners. As the Depression worsened, trade diminished into an international trade war.

What made things different than in previous economic downturns? The US economy had become more integrated with Europe. To be sure, the twenties saw nowhere near the level of integration that we see in the twenty-first century, but it had increased. During World War I the United States had assumed the role of the dominant financial center. The system of reparations and debt payment depended on the international flow of gold, finance, and trade. US trade suffered as other countries raised tariffs in retaliation. On May 8 the Federal Reserve Board acknowledged that the country had slipped into a depression.

As an illustration of the extent to which the normal rules no longer applied, it would have been logical for an investor to enter the market at the low point of 1930. The brief rally would have supported that strategy. However, buying low at this moment in time would not have worked. The stock market would not recover for years.

The Banking Crisis

The recession of 1929–30 did not initially appear to be worse than any other recession, certainly not something on the scale of the Great Depression. This is where a great deal of the subsequent contentious debate takes place. Did the policy reaction, or lack thereof, make matters worse? Scholars argue over what relation, if any, the crash has to the Depression. Just as the crash surprised many, the subsequent Depression also proved unexpected. As noted earlier Keynes and Fisher, two of the leading economists in the world, both believed the crisis had passed by April 1930. The next part of the story takes place away from Wall Street in other avenues of the banking industry.

From December to October 1931 a series of bank panics, beginning with the New York Bank of the United States, swept the country. Despite its name the Bank of the United States had no affiliation with the US government. Founded by Joseph S. Marcus, a Jewish immigrant, in 1913, the bank catered to immigrants and the working class. Some speculated that the bank's name served to deceive depositors into thinking the bank was affiliated with the US Treasury. In 1919 Bernard Marcus took his father's place at the head of the bank and expanded it rapidly. Prospering during the twenties, by 1930 it reached a large enough size that its failure created widespread problems.

In December 1931 a crowd formed outside the Bronx branch to withdraw deposits. This bank run might have started the Great Depression. Monetarists argue that the Federal Reserve should have intervened to save the Bank of the United States. As runs began at other branches, the directors closed the bank, with plans to reopen it. However, during the closure the New York State Bureau of Securities announced an investigation of the bank, and the Bank of the United States collapsed. Immigrant and working-class depositors lost $200 million in assets in one of the largest bank failures in US history. It

A crowd formed outside the Bank of the United States demanding their money, a bank run some believed helped trigger the wave of bank failures that contributed to the Depression. Despite the bank's name, the national government had no affiliation with it. Neither the Federal Reserve Board nor a bankers' pool bailed out the bank. *Source:* Library of Congress, New York World-Telegram & Sun Collection, http://hdl.loc.gov/loc.pnp/cph.3c17261 (public domain).

is not clear why the Federal Reserve or other banks did not rescue the Bank of the United States, since banks had long used the old method of a banking clearinghouse to provide liquidity. The establishment banks might have been reluctant to help the Jewish and working class. It might also be the case that bankers assumed the Federal Reserve Board would act as the lender of last resort, which it failed to do. The Bank of the United States' failure reverberated throughout the financial sector.

The failure of the Bank of the United States triggered what would be the first of three waves of bank failures. At this time the banking system in the United States had many small banks that were vulnerable to runs. Convoluted state laws limited the size of banks or the number of branches a bank could have. These bank failures resulted in a sharp contraction in the money supply and a freezing of liquidity that the Federal Reserve Board could not counter. The banking crisis became an international crisis. Remember that an English bank had already failed. In May 1931 the Kredit-Anstalt, Austria's largest bank, defaulted. This fed into the general difficulties with international finance left over from World War I. J. P. Morgan and Company, with some other inter-

national banks, had floated German bonds that would be used to pay reparations, which the British and French would use to pay war debt. The Austrian
failure created a fear that Germany would default on its debts.

Beginning in June and running through December 1931, a second wave of
bank failures swept the United States. The collapse of Wall Street, the worsening US economy, and slumping trade exacerbated problems with the British and European economies. The British had not fully recovered from World
War I when the Depression hit, and the resulting contraction in the money
supply is what prompted Britain to leave the gold standard in September
1931. British abandonment of the gold standard came as a shock. The Bank
of England, the Federal Reserve Board, and J. P. Morgan and Company had
all worked throughout the 1920s to restore and reinforce the gold standard.
Winston Churchill, as chancellor of the exchequer, had returned Britain to
the gold standard in 1925, pegging the pound at its prewar levels. This proved
to be a disaster for British exports. Abandoning the gold standard allowed
Britain to have a flexible currency and inflate its way out of the deflationary
cycle. Leaving the gold standard put Britain on the path to recovery.

At this point the US economy hit the "double bottom," a point that Hoover
made in his memoir. The money supply contracted and the Consumer Price
Index fell 9.4 percent. In August 1931 Hoover created the President's Emergency Committee for Employment (later the President's Organization for
Unemployment Relief) to coordinate local welfare agencies. Despite the ex-
pansions of the government during the Progressive Era and World War I, the
federal government did not have an extensive bureaucracy or a social safety
net. As the Depression settled in, Hoover called for public works, such as the
construction of the Hoover Dam, and for tax cuts. The difficulty with the tax
cuts is that the federal income taxes were, at this time, a relatively small part
of the economy, so cutting taxes in half did not free up sufficient additional
income. By 1932 Hoover prepared to take additional action. In January 1932
Congress created the Reconstruction Finance Corporation (RFC). The RFC
lent money to banks, insurance companies, railroads, and similar businesses.
Critics referred to it as the "millionaire's dole." The Glass-Steagall Act of 1932
made credit easier to obtain by releasing $750 million in gold from the Fed-
eral Reserve. The Emergency Relief and Construction Act provided loans to
states and money to state and local governments for relief work.

By the summer of 1932 the economy was showing some signs of recovery
when a third wave of bank failures hit. One-third of US banks were either

closed or taken over. This banking crisis, however, would be tackled by a new president, Franklin D. Roosevelt.

Did the Crash Cause the Great Depression?

October 1929 stands as a breaking point between the prosperity of the 1920s and the Depression of the 1930s. The real question is not whether the stock market crash traumatized the nation. It did. The October 1929 crash shocked the system, especially the financial system. Descriptions of Wall Street in the aftermath painted a bleak picture. During the crash exhausted clerks and brokers desperately tried to keep up with events. Then Wall Street became a ghost town. During the 1920s Wall Street bustled with power and influence. During the 1930s it was a shadow of its former self, as influence and power moved to New Deal–era Washington, DC. There is wisdom in Frederick Lewis Allen's statement that "prosperity is more than an economic condition, it is a state of mind."[14] The October 1929 crash broke the psychology of prosperity. Even if the Great Depression had not emerged, the age of easy progress and change equating with modernity ended. The crash may not have caused the recession or Depression, but it got the ball rolling.

As has been noted, various schools of thought, particularly among economists, exist as to what caused the Depression and to what extent, if any, the stock market crash caused it. The list of items singled out as possible causes is impressive and speaks to the complexity of the problem: overconsumption, overproduction, too much debt, too loose a currency, the gold standard, reparations, high tariffs, too much government, not enough government, and so forth. There is also debate over when the Depression began, a debate that is informed by what part of the economy one looks at. For example, followers of the Austrian School believe the Depression was a necessary correction to the overly aggressive expansion of the money supply during the 1920s, which government policies prolonged by interfering with the market correction. Keynesians see the Depression primarily as a problem of demand, that workers lacked sufficient income to purchase goods. Others see it as a supply-side issue, that too much had been produced. Many of these theories are contingent on "what if" scenarios. John Kenneth Galbraith, a Keynesian, focused on institutional issues in his classic *The Great Crash, 1929*. He noted predictors of the depth of the Depression: supply of money combined with the actions of the Federal Reserve Board and flaws in the structure of the interwar gold standard. While economists disagree as to the linkage between the stock market crash and the onset of the Depression, it is fair to say that the crash rattled consumers' faith in the future and, quite possibly, hindered their ability to consume goods. The stock market crash signaled the beginning of an intense deflationary cycle, during which falling prices discouraged consumption and many people found that they lacked the money to purchase the necessities of life. There was poverty amidst plenty.

Conditions of the Great Depression

In the summer of 1932 you could have found yourself at the movies. Legend has it that Hollywood did well during the Depression, and there is truth to the story. The film industry transformed from one of the golden icons of 1920s modernity into an industry that helped Americans forget their woes. At first, the Depression hit Hollywood hard, but it rebounded. Movies provided an inexpensive diversion from everyday life. For about a quarter a person could catch a popular screwball comedy, a movie genre that began during the Depression. Preston Sturges's movie, *Sullivan's Travels* (1941), captures the appeal of the Depression-era comedies. In the film, set in the Depression and somewhat autobiographical, a successful director tires of making light-hearted fluff, wanting to make an artistic film that reflects grim reality. He leaves his mansion to travel as a hobo. However, in the end he discovers the value of making people laugh as a way of forgetting life's travails.

You might also have seen a Frank Capra film. Capra, an enormously popular director, made comedies such as *It Happened One Night* (1934), *You Can't Take It with You* (1938), and *Arsenic and Old Lace* (1944), but also more politically charged films such as *Mr. Smith Goes to Washington* (1939) and *Meet John Doe* (1941), not to mention *It's a Wonderful Life* (1946). Capra warned that Depression conditions threatened American democracy as people became more desperate, and more radical. The rise of fascism and communism in Europe was not lost on this Italian immigrant.

The highest-grossing films of the decade were musicals, *Gold Diggers of 1933* (1933), *42nd Street* (1933), and *Footlight Parade* (1933), which involved people from all social classes joining together. *Gold Diggers of 1933* features an old-money millionaire who agrees to back a Broadway production that saves unemployed choir girls. *42nd Street* also features a wealthy man who sponsors a play. In the *Wizard of Oz* (1939) audiences saw Dorothy transported from the depressed state of Kansas to a magical land where she learns to work with others and, ultimately, finds the value in returning home. Popular gangster movies reflected the tensions of the decade, often depicting ethnic Americans in their struggle to gain a foothold in the United States, with a hint of defiance tending toward a Robin Hood theme. *The Public Enemy* (1931) depicts a family torn apart by illegal activity, especially during Prohibition. *Little Caesar* (1931) gave Edward G. Robinson his first role as a gangster, who rises to the top of the mob. *Scarface* (1932) depicts a crime syndicate specializing in bootleg booze.

Prior to the movie, one caught a cartoon and a newsreel. The newsreel would have presented a stark contrast to a light-hearted screwball comedy. The newsreels might have highlighted the 6,000 or so unemployed people in New York City reduced to selling apples for a nickel. Selling apples symbolized Depression-era unemployment. One might also have seen soup kitchens feeding the unemployed but also noticed that the poor in need of a meal were dressed in worn and tattered business suits, a remnant of their success during the 1920s and now a familiar sight on Wall Street.

Some raw statistics indicate how bad the economy became. Even given the vagaries of economic data at the time, and that unemployment was calculated differently from today, the data still paint a striking picture. In August 1929 the unemployment rate stood at 3 percent. By March 1933 it stood at 25 percent. That figure is somewhat deceptive because it doesn't reflect regional and industry variations. The unemployment rate was much higher and lower in some places. Of course, some of the underemployed wanted to work full time. Some firms limited hours in the hope of preserving jobs. As the Depression unfolded, businesses would fire, or refuse to hire, women to save jobs for men, on the assumption that men supported families. As the Depression continued, women's lower wages looked more attractive to employers. Let's now take another set of numbers. The Industrial Production Index stood at 114 in August 1929, but by March 1933 it was 54. The Federal Reserve Board released the index as a measure of manufacturing and similar industries. Dropping by over half reflected a crisis in manufacturing.

In light of these dire conditions, in January 1931, Congressman Wright Patman introduced what became known as the "Bonus Bill," in which he proposed that a bonus promised to World War I veterans be paid immediately. Congress had first passed bonus legislation in the early 1920s, but President Warren Harding vetoed it in the name of financial austerity. Congress passed it again, eventually overriding Calvin Coolidge's veto in 1924. The Bonus Act allocated each veteran $1 for each day served domestically and $1.25 for each day served abroad. The bonus, however, would not be due for some time, and veterans wanted the money right away, during the Depression. Hoover opposed paying the bonus early, on the grounds that it would cost $4 billion even as, in February 1931, food riots broke out in cities. Other cities began experimenting with issuing currency or running on a barter system because of the lack of currency. Conditions continued to deteriorate. In March 1931 workers at Ford's River Rouge plant marched in protest. Dearborn police attacked the protestors, killing four. During April 1932, 750,000 unemployed (with more on a waiting list) depended on New York City relief, which paid $8.20 per month.

In June 1932 the Bonus Expeditionary Force arrived in Washington, DC. Along with friends and family, thousands of World War I veterans camped in Hoovervilles in Anacostia Flats. Patman's Bonus Bill had passed the House but failed in the Senate. The bonus marches intended to pressure Congress to pass the bill. Paying the bonus, however, would run counter to the desire for a balanced budget and individual responsibility. Rather than support the Bonus Bill, Hoover signed legislation providing $100,000 to transport the Bonus Army home. He gave the Bonus Army a July 24 deadline to leave the capital. On July 28 the attorney general had the police remove the marchers, but they returned. Hoover then ordered the Army, under the command of General Douglas MacArthur, to remove the marchers. MacArthur, accusing them of being communist revolutionaries, moved in with tear gas and tanks, burning the Hoovervilles, which provided stark images for the newsreels. Removing the Bonus Army was a political disaster for Hoover.

As Hoover's political fortunes declined, he attempted to be creative. Despite his denial of the bonus, in fact, he became one of the most activist presidents to date, convinced that more needed to be done. In July 1932 he authorized the Reconstruction Finance Corporation to lend states money for relief and public works. Deflation continued as the Consumer Price Index fell a combined 16.2 percent from 1932 to 1933. Hoover lost control of the situation, and the man known for his ability to manage his image retreated into the White House. The economy bottomed out in March 1933, the same month Franklin D. Roosevelt was sworn in as president of the United States.

Generations removed from the crash and the Depression, it is important to remember that at the time, particularly for those with money in banks and the markets, the crash was a traumatic event that shaped the experience of a generation. At the time of the crash, it was almost universally assumed that the crash was a direct cause of the Depression and for some, at least, represented the failure of capitalism. Those who responded to the crash and Depression did not have a guidebook. While, after the fact, it is worthwhile for academics to focus on a single cause, leaders had to act in the economic equivalent of the fog of war, considering not only the economic but political and social implications of their actions. Living in the United States, it can be easy to forget that the Depression decade saw the rise of totalitarian states and extreme ideologies such as fascism.

5 How the New Deal Changed the Financial Sector

Out with the Old

AT THE 1933 presidential inauguration, Herbert Hoover rode in an automobile with Franklin Roosevelt, looking obviously unhappy; this produced one of the most famous pictures in American politics. The man Calvin Coolidge called the "Wonder Boy," the man who searched for problems to solve, found the crisis he could not solve. The Depression defeated Hoover, and now Roosevelt would tackle it. Later scholars argued that Hoover did not pursue staunchly conservative policies, but rather policies that foreshadowed Roosevelt's New Deal. However, in 1933 Hoover feared that Roosevelt would lead the nation in radical experimentation that would endanger his beloved American individualism. Years of depression economics increased the appeal of radical politics. Ideologues argued that capitalism had failed. Communists and fascists mobilized in Europe. The unemployed desperately called for solutions to the economic crisis. However, there existed no clear path to prosperity. In response, Roosevelt responded with economic experimentation and optimistic leadership.

Although in retrospect we see Franklin Roosevelt as a very liberal or progressive president, that is perhaps not the most useful way of looking at Roosevelt's New Deal policies. Roosevelt and the New Dealers clearly identified with the political left, but FDR often infuriated his advisors with his willingness to experiment and try new things. They urged Roosevelt to nationalize the banking system. Instead, he embarked on a sometimes contradictory set of New Deal policies, emphasizing the "three Rs": relief, recovery, and reform. For relief New Deal agencies created thousands of government jobs for the unemployed that injected money into the economy. For recovery the New Deal embarked on a period of economic planning and emphasized cooperation between government, business, and labor. The economy grew, but not enough to end the Depression. New Dealers reformed the banking and financial industries to prevent another Depression. Roosevelt signed legislation creating new agencies, the Security and Exchange Commission and the Federal Deposit Insurance Corporation. Banking reform also separated commercial banking from investment banking. Banks could no longer speculate with depositors' money. New Dealers wanted to prevent another bubble and to shield the public from the negative consequences of speculating.

It would be Roosevelt, not Hoover, who tackled reforming the financial crisis and got political credit for fighting the Depression. The Great Depression brought a sea change to American politics that reinforced the competing views of finance and industrialization, which went back to Jefferson and Hamilton and had fueled the Progressive Era debate over the money trust. Louis Brandeis, author of *Other People's Money* and the progressive foe of centralized financial power, became an unofficial advisor to the New Dealers. The result of Roosevelt's negotiation of the economics and politics of the Depression is a baffling array of initiatives and agencies that forever changed the role of the government in American society and economics.

The Technocrat and the Politician: Hoover and FDR

Observers like to comment on the characters of Hoover and FDR. There is fairness to this, because the personalities of the two men had an impact on their style of leadership and the psychology of the Depression. Hoover, the self-made man, lost the ability to empathize with the suffering of people, while Roosevelt, a sheltered child of privilege, ushered in an age when people expected a president to understand and address their suffering.

Economic bubbles often bring the discussion back to the relationship between private gain and public risk. One of the ironies—tragedies, really—of Herbert Hoover is that he gave serious thought to the relationship between the public and the private, individuality and society. The tragedy is compounded when we take into account his private misgivings about speculation in the stock market. Hoover walked a fine line between rugged individualism and cooperative action. While it is true that Hoover bitterly attacked the New Deal after his presidency, this obscures the fact that, during his tenure as secretary of commerce and president, Hoover fell more into the camp of Hamilton than Jefferson. Hoover saw the future in planning, only he believed that private citizens and business should lead the way, not the government. The government could, and would, play a constructive probusiness role in the economy that fostered cooperation between private institutions.

During the Depression, Hoover's strength became his liability. Americans elected Hoover on his technocratic prowess. He was the Great Engineer, who lacked partisan loyalties, but during the Depression he seemed politically tone-deaf. In 1920 Franklin Roosevelt championed Hoover as a Democratic nominee for president until Hoover declared as a Republican. In retrospect, Roosevelt's endorsement of Hoover is intensely ironic; Roosevelt praised the man he would later soundly defeat and repudiate. However, in 1920 it made sense. Hoover had served in Woodrow Wilson's administration and supported Teddy Roosevelt's Bull Moose Party. For Hoover, the common good meant having the government promote business and particularly cooperation, not competition, between businesses. Hoover pursued this vision, his Associational State, vigorously as secretary of commerce. Hoover saw himself as a champion of New Era economic modernization, not partisan politics.

Hoover understood that Wall Street speculation would probably not end well. Despite his public New Era boosterism, within the Coolidge administration Hoover warned against the danger of a stock market bubble and advocated for intervention to prevent it. Likewise, Hoover understood that the United States should not ignore Europe's economic difficulties left over from World War I. As it turned out, Hoover's presidency turned on his ability to handle the economic crisis that both events had contributed to. Hoover had a demonstrated, successful record using a public office to rally individuals and private companies to deal with a crisis. On paper, Herbert Hoover should have been a great president. Rather, he left office highly unpopular, viewed as a failure overshadowed by Roosevelt and his New Deal.

In 1928 voters did not see Hoover as an ideologue but as the embodiment of the technocratic expertise of the businessman. Hoover seemed a perfect match for the heyday of the gentleman banker. It is with some irony then, that Herbert Hoover would leave office unpopular and would spend the next three decades (he died in 1964 at the age of ninety) as a bitter critic of the New Deal and government planning in the economy. Scholars now argue that Hoover's creations, the Reconstruction Finance Corporation and public works such as the Hoover Dam, foreshadowed the New Deal.

Franklin D. Roosevelt's aristocratic lifestyle contrasted sharply with Hoover's biography. Hoover came from a modest background, the son of a Quaker blacksmith who attended the first class at Standard University to study mining engineering. By contrast, Franklin Roosevelt came from old money. During his presidency, the wealthy, chief among them J. P. Morgan, considered Roosevelt a "class traitor." Morgan carried a deep grudge against the New Dealers for perceived slights during congressional hearings on the crash. Even Hoover's critics regarded Hoover as intelligent. Some doubted Roosevelt's intelligence, instead citing his "first class character" as his best gift. Both men admired Teddy Roosevelt, but FDR counted the former president as family.

If one looks at Roosevelt's biography going into his late thirties, it isn't necessarily surprising that be became president, but it is surprising that he would become a president whom millions of Americans expected to understand their problems and would personally appeal to for aid. FDR had a privileged childhood on his family's Hudson Valley estate at Hyde Park, where private tutors oversaw his education until he left to attend Groton Academy. Groton was a boarding and preparatory school founded by Rev. Endicott Peabody, a relation to the Peabody who had given Junius Morgan entry into London finance, thereby setting the stage for the rise of the House of Morgan. Roosevelt then attended Harvard, where he earned gentleman's Cs and began but did not complete Columbia Law School, preferring instead to pass the bar. In 1905 he married Eleanor Roosevelt, a distant cousin. President Teddy Roosevelt gave away the bride. A few years of practicing law convinced FDR that he needed to find another line of work, so he entered politics. In 1910 he won his first election, becoming a New York state senator. During World War I Roosevelt served as Wilson's assistant secretary of the Navy, in the same administration in which Hoover served as food administrator and as part of the delegation to the Treaty of Versailles negotiations. In 1920 the Democrats nominated Roosevelt as the vice presidential candidate, running on the ticket with James

Cox, the ticket that lost to Warren G. Harding and Calvin Coolidge. By his late thirties Democratic leaders had high expectations for Franklin Roosevelt. He seemed to be following in his cousin Teddy's footsteps. He also, however, had a reputation for being callow. How is it that this most patrician of men became the political voice of the common people?

While this is another question where a precise answer cannot be known, it is likely that Roosevelt's experience with polio transformed him. At the age of thirty-nine, in the summer of 1921, Roosevelt visited Campobello Island, where he contracted polio. Roosevelt would never walk again without aid. Loss of the use of his legs, seemingly, meant the end of his political career. FDR retired to Hyde Park to recuperate while Eleanor Roosevelt and Louis Howe politicked in his name. Roosevelt's biographers consider his battle with polio key to understanding his leadership during the Great Depression. Hoover retreated into the White House as the Depression worsened, whereas Roosevelt had to make an effort to leave his house. During his recuperation Roosevelt learned to maintain his optimism and patience; he never stopped trying to cure his paralysis. He was forced to rely on surrogates, such as Eleanor, to do many of the functions that politicians normally do. FDR could not work a crowd; rather, he became a master of the radio. He supported New York governor Al Smith, including his unsuccessful 1924 bid for the Democratic nomination. In 1928 Smith became the Democratic presidential nominee, losing to Hoover. That same year Smith encouraged Roosevelt to run for governor in New York, which he did, successfully bucking a Republican tide and marking Roosevelt's comeback from polio.

Roosevelt had been in office for only a short time when the stock market crashed, after which he and his advisors previewed on the state level much of what would become the New Deal. Roosevelt courted intellectuals and academics, his brain trust. He enjoyed hearing conflicting points of view. He also enjoyed defying conventional wisdom. He lowered taxes, supported public power initiatives and public works to provide relief for the unemployed. As a result, voters reelected Roosevelt in 1930 (New York governors served two-year terms at that time), propelling him into front-runner status for the Democratic presidential nomination.

Happy Days Are Here Again

Just as we imagined how an average investor might view Wall Street in the 1920s, we might now take a few moments to consider how the election might look to the average voter. As we have established, it would have been difficult for the situation to be grimmer. The Great Depression entered its worst period, with seemingly no end in sight. Hoover had tried to convince the country that things would turn around, but he had failed dismally. Roosevelt, by contrast, embodied optimism. Even though he had kept his paralysis a secret, the public knew that he had overcome illness to reenter politics. More than a few commented that Roosevelt's physical recovery would serve as a model for the nation's recovery. The two candidates offered dramatically different personalities, but how did they differ on the issues? A voter in 1932 would have had a hard time determining how Roosevelt's policies would differ from Hoover's.

To Hoover's enormous frustration Roosevelt offered vague and contradictory statements on the campaign trail. Roosevelt understood he could easily win the election, so he set out to not lose it. Roosevelt promised change. Beyond that, he remained vague, but voters knew they did not want Hoover. At the Democratic National Convention in Chicago, Roosevelt broke tradition by accepting the nomination in person. Prior to this, presidential candidates stayed home, orchestrating their nomination campaigns from afar through proxies, all the while pretending they were not running for president. After the party nominated a candidate, it would arrange a ceremony later, furthering the pretense that the candidate had not sought out the nomination. As the convention started, Roosevelt stayed at Hyde Park, telephoning his lieutenants. When it became clear he would win the nomination, he boarded a plane for Chicago on a stormy night. Roosevelt, walking out on stage, thanks to his concealed leg braces, helped put to rest concerns that he lacked the health to lead the country. Roosevelt's willingness to take risks offers insight into his presidency. First of all, his flight to Chicago went through a dangerous storm. Secondly, for Roosevelt to "walk" onstage meant taking a risk of falling, effectively ending his presidential bid.

His acceptance speech is not noted for his policy recommendations, but rather for breaking the "absurd tradition" that the nominee "should remain in professed ignorance" of his nomination, just as the country now needed to "break foolish traditions" such as those, he argued, that the Republicans upheld. Doing away with pretense indicated his "intention to be honest and avoid all hypocrisy or sham, to avoid all shutting of the eyes to the truth in this campaign." Roosevelt pointed out that the Depression brought the danger of "wild radicalism," but he advocated combating radicalism not with conservative reaction but with "a workable program of reconstruction." Reform would stymie revolution. Roosevelt then laid out the debate as he saw it: "There are two ways of viewing the Government's duty in matters affecting economic and social life. The first sees to it that a favored few are helped and hopes that some of their prosperity will leak through, sift through, to labor, to the farmer, to the small business man. That theory belongs to the party of Toryism, and I had hoped that most of the Tories left this country in 1776." In contrast, the Democratic Party "must be a party of liberal thought, of planned action, of enlightened international outlook, and of the greatest good to the greatest number of our citizens."[1]

Roosevelt subscribed to the surplus production theory as to the causes of the Depression. Throughout the 1920s, he explained, profits increased while consumers saw little drop in prices and workers saw little increase in wages. As a result, factories amassed a large surplus of goods. Roosevelt offered a series of policy proposals that included reducing government waste, lowering taxes, repealing Prohibition, aiding farmers, lowering tariffs to increase trade, and creating public works for the unemployed. As policy, few of the New Deal initiatives were completely new. Hoover had tried several of them. Roosevelt, however, differed in his underlying philosophy. As he explained, "Our Republican leaders tell us economic laws—sacred, inviolable, unchangeable—cause panics which no one could prevent. But while they prate of economic laws, men and women are starving. We must lay hold of the fact that economic laws are not made by nature. They are made by human beings." Roosevelt concluded with a flourish that became the signature theme of the campaign, "I pledge you, I pledge myself, to a new deal for the American people. Let us all here assembled constitute ourselves prophets of a new order of competence and of courage. This is more than a political campaign; it is a call to arms. Give me your help, not to win votes alone, but to win in this crusade to restore America to its own people."[2] As Roosevelt finished his speech, the campaign's theme song, "Happy Days Are Here Again," began. With the economy in shambles, voters looked to Roosevelt for optimism and relief, not for consistent policies. Roosevelt and the Democrats won in a landslide.

The Banking Crisis Redux

As discussed in the previous chapter, Hoover's term saw not only the stock market crash but waves of bank failures. Another of the banking crises began in the waning days of Hoover's administration. Roosevelt won the election in

November but would not take office until March. Hoover was a lame-duck president during the interim. These four months saw another wave of bank failures. The financial system teetered on the brink of complete collapse. Bank runs became commonplace. About a third of the banking system failed. Beginning in Michigan, governors took action by declaring a banking holiday. During a banking holiday, the government closed all the banks in order to stop panic-driven bank runs and to allow auditors to shore up the system. Hoover considered a nationwide bank holiday but felt constrained by having just lost the election. He wanted Roosevelt to endorse his actions. Why would Hoover do this? In part, Hoover had lost credibility. He had tried, without success, to restore confidence to the economy. His endorsement of a plan would carry little weight and might even damage the plan. Hoover also feared that Roosevelt would do something radical, such as nationalize the banking system. He wanted to limit the incoming president's options. Roosevelt, realizing that any action endorsed by Hoover would be tainted, refused to cooperate.

No national actions would be taken to deal with the banking crisis until Roosevelt took office in March 1933. His inauguration corresponded with the economy bottoming out. The nation faced a severe deflationary cycle, where prices continued to fall, eroding wages and earnings. Unemployment stood at 25 percent. A shortage of currency and credit hampered the economy. Perhaps more than anything else, few people had confidence that the economy would recover. Traditionally, the president-elect and first lady rode in the augural parade with the outgoing president and his wife. Hoover embodied the picture of dejection, a reflection of a grim time. By contrast, Roosevelt projected self-confidence with his jutting chin and uplifted cigarette. He beamed confidence next to a gloomy Hoover. In his inaugural address, which Roosevelt wrote, the new president directly addressed the nation's psychological state: "We have nothing to fear, but fear itself." To impress upon the public the vigor with which he would combat the crisis, Roosevelt evoked World War I. Fighting the Depression would be as critical as fighting a war and require the same level of governmental power. Roosevelt promised bold experimentation. His inaugural stands as one of the high-water marks in presidential leadership. With the speech Roosevelt did not fix the economy, but he did address the psychology of the Depression, the general lack of confidence. Just as manias and panics are fueled by mob mentalities, recoveries can be fueled by a positive belief in the future. However, it would take more than Roosevelt's optimism to lift the nation out of the Depression.

The Banking Acts: How Roosevelt's Leadership Worked

When he took office, Roosevelt declared a nationwide bank holiday, using an obscure clause in the Espionage Act, which dated to World War I. Roosevelt's advisors made many policy suggestions, including replacing the dollar as the national currency and nationalizing the banking system. The longer Roosevelt left the banks closed, the more he risked total economic meltdown. People could not access their bank accounts. They only had whatever currency they kept on themselves or in their homes. A barter system arose in parts of the country. However, if unsound banks reopened and failed, the bank runs would resume.

One of the issues that the New Dealers confronted was that they began work amidst an extraordinary emergency. Roosevelt appointees entered their offices as the emergency unfolded. In a bipartisan act Roosevelt's partially assembled administration worked with Treasury Department officials held over from the Hoover administration to craft legislation. Roosevelt would make use of initiatives that Hoover administration people had been working on. Working side by side, the Hoover and Roosevelt appointees crafted the response to the banking crisis that became the Banking Act of 1933. Incredibly, Congress passed the legislation within a few hours. The speaker of the house used a rolled-up newspaper as proxy for the bill.

Meanwhile, Roosevelt delivered the first of his fireside chats. As we saw with our discussion of the New Era economy, radio transformed politics. Although Hoover, as secretary of commerce, had embraced the radio and had recognized the need for the government to allocate airwaves, as president he did not successfully use the radio. Roosevelt turned out to be a natural on the radio who took full advantage of his ability to speak directly to the people. With his fireside chats he could reach directly into voters' homes. In addressing the banking crisis, he took a soothing, reassuring tone as he explained how banks worked and announced the nationwide bank holiday. The public needed to be reassured, not only to end the panics and bank runs, but also to allow the bank holiday to work. Once again, mass psychology came into play. In closing the banks, Roosevelt took a big step. Some governors had already closed the banks within their states, but Roosevelt now took the step nationwide. Using emergency powers left over from World War I, the president closed every bank in the United States. Critically, the government needed to act to restore the system, because no banking took place, no loans,

Like his father, the younger J. P. Morgan testified before a congressional commit-
tee regarding a stock market crash. The younger Morgan lacked his father's gravitas
and, following the banking acts, became a leading critic of the New Deal.
Source: US Information Agency, Series: Photographic File of the Paris Bureau of the
New York Times, compiled ca. 1900–ca. 1950, Record Group 306: Records of the
US Information Agency, 1900–2003 (public domain).

no withdrawals, and for some, no access to money. During the bank holiday,
government auditors would go through the banks, closing unsound banks and
reopening sound ones. Remarkably, when the banks reopened people lined
up to deposit money.

Roosevelt's fireside chat dealt with the immediate crisis, but not its causes.
The administration also had to find a long-term solution to the problem of
banking panics. It found help in congressional hearings, which captivated the
nation and opened the banking process to public scrutiny.

The Pecora Commission

On March 4, 1932, the US Senate Committee on Banking and Currency
began hearings on the stock market crash of 1929. The hearings built on the
momentum of the public's outrage over the crash and Depression. Beginning
in April, the investigation took on new life, when the Democrats assumed
control of the Senate. Chief Council Ferdinand Pecora was an Italian immigrant, a former assistant district attorney, and a political foe of Tammany Hall.

He had supported Teddy Roosevelt's Bull Moose Party and then switched to the Democratic Party to support Woodrow Wilson. Pecora became the face of the investigations, even appearing on the cover of *Time* magazine. Pecora thoroughly investigated Wall Street, calling before the committee some of the biggest names in banking, including Richard Whitney, now president of the NYSE, his brother and Morgan partner George Whitney, Morgan partner Thomas Lamont, Otto Kahn, Albert H. Wiggin of Chase National Bank, and Charles E. Mitchell of National City Bank.

The Pecora Commission's findings seemingly confirmed the public's suspicion that Wall Street was a rigged casino. The committee revealed that Albert Wiggin, who had committed Chase National Bank to the pool that attempted to stop the stock market crash, had also been short selling shares in Chase since September 1929. Wiggin made over $4 million betting against the bank he ran. Senator Carter Glass said Charles "Sunshine Charlie" Mitchell "more than forty others is responsible for the present trouble."[3] Mitchell's New Era bullishness knew few limits, to the point where he had undermined the Federal Reserve's efforts to slow down speculation. In addition to his actions with the Federal Reserve, National City Bank had repackaged bad Latin American loans as securities and sold them to investors looking for a safe investment. Now, in the wake of the bursting bubble Mitchell came under fire for tax evasion and losing millions of dollars for investors.

Pecora, as the face of the investigation, created a narrative that pitted immigrants and ethnic Americans, who would become an important part of the New Deal coalition, against the old guard of Wall Street. In some ways the hearings recreated the old ethnic and religious tensions from Wall Street. The hearings also brought into the light of day the opaque and secretive world of the bankers. Despite the celebrity bankers had achieved during the 1920s, finance and banking remained a highly convoluted system marked by confidentiality and an insider's network. No institution represented the old guard better than J. P. Morgan and Company. For the first time its books and practices would be open to outsiders.

When called before the committee, Jack Morgan walked in his father's footsteps. The senior Morgan's testimony before the Pujo Committee's investigation into the Panic of 1907 had been a virtuoso performance, a full-throated defense of private banking conducted by gentlemen. Indeed, although often vilified by political opponents, within the banking world Morgan and his partners prided themselves on high-minded business practices. The younger

Morgan, shy and disliking public appearances, could not muster the level of gravitas of his father. Rather, he came across as old fashioned and out of date, his defense of banking amounted to the argument that J. P. Morgan and Company did business the high-minded way and should be trusted. Morgan concluded "that I consider the private banker a national asset and not a national danger."[4]

The national mood had changed considerably. Now senators insisted, for the first time ever, that J. P. Morgan and Company open its books for inspection. The information stunned the public. Morgan partners sat not only on the boards of other companies but also on the boards of other banks. The company maintained a preferred list of customers, who had access to secret options to buy securities at a discount. For example, a preferred customer might be offered so many shares at $20 with the knowledge that the share would probably bring $35 when sold to the general investing public. Members of the preferred list included former president Calvin Coolidge, members of Congress, the secretary of the treasury, and the former head of the Democratic National Committee. J. P. Morgan and his partners paid no income tax for 1930 through 1931 due to heavy losses in 1929, but it still looked bad. Carter Glass stated that the hearings looked like "a circus." Inspired by his comment, the Ringling Bros. circus decided to have a female dwarf performer approach Morgan after his testimony. The woman sitting on Morgan's lap became one of the iconic pictures of the Depression.

Following the hearings Morgan became a bitter opponent of Franklin Roosevelt and the New Deal. Morgan felt that Roosevelt and the New Dealers had treated him and the banks unfairly. Unfairly or not, as a result of the public outrage over the revelations, Congress passed the Banking Act of 1933, the Securities Act of 1933, and the Securities Exchange Act of 1934. This legislation substantially changed the financial world, effectively ending the gentleman's banking club that J. P. Morgan and Company represented.

The Glass-Steagall Act

The Banking Act of 1933, commonly known as the Glass-Steagall Act, would have a profound impact on banking for generations. The act had two significant parts. First, it separated commercial from investment banking. The idea being that commercial banks should not be able to use deposits, other people's money, to take investment risks. That is, bank deposits should not be used as call loans. Investment banking would be lucrative, but riskier.

Second, the act created the Federal Deposit Insurance Corporation (FDIC). The FDIC insured bank deposits, removing the reason for bank runs and panics. Banks would buy insurance from a government agency that insured deposits, so depositors knew their money would be safe in the event of a failure. However, Roosevelt initially opposed the FDIC, for fear that it would encourage banks to take greater risks, knowing that the government would replace lost money. This is not unlike the Federal Reserve acting as the lender of last resort. In both instances the concern is that the penalty for risky behavior is removed from the bankers and transferred to the tax-paying public. Bankers would feel freer to risk depositors' money. Roosevelt, however, acquiesced to deposit insurance. In response to the act, Wall Street engaged in a short strike, as agents refused to bring new issues to market.

The Securities Act of 1933, also known as the Truth in Securities Act, mandated that sales of securities be reported to the Securities and Exchange Commission. Congress justified this law under the Interstate Commerce Clause of the Constitution. Prior to this act, individual states regulated securities with Blue Sky Laws, the same laws that had troubled Ivar Kreuger. Blue Sky Laws often had specific requirements for a security to be sold within a state. In other words, under Blue Sky Laws a state government determined the merit of an investment. In contracts, the act mandated that a security be registered with the SEC in a process that required the disclosure of relevant information to investors making the decision, rather than establishing standards for a security. Under the act, the agency selling the securities had to provide a great deal of information, a process called "due diligence," and was liable for not providing accurate information. However, an investor could still make a bad investment. Under the act, the government did not attempt to judge the merit of the investment but rather to give the investor the information to make the judgment.

The Securities Exchange Act created the Securities and Exchange Commission, commonly referred to as the SEC, which regulates the sale of securities. Congress gave the SEC broad regulatory powers to "register, regulate, and oversee" securities, including brokerage firms, transfer agents, and clearing agencies. The SEC became the regulatory body that oversaw stock exchanges, such as the NYSE and the NASDAQ. The act also made insider trading illegal, and it did away with many of the practices that had defined the financial industry. No longer could gentlemen arrange preferred lists or count on their banks' records remaining secret.

To head the new SEC, Roosevelt appointed Joseph Kennedy. Kennedy's reputation as a stock manipulator on Wall Street made him something of a surprise selection. The son-in-law of a well-known Democratic mayor of Boston had connections to the Democratic Party. Kennedy had made a fortune in the stock market, in part by engaging in insider trading and market manipulations, the very practices now outlawed. Roosevelt countered critics of Kennedy's appointment by asking who knew these tactics better than Kennedy. Rumor had it that Kennedy sold his shares just before the crash and made more money short selling during the crash. Somewhat famously, Kennedy said that when a shoeshine boy gave him stock tips he knew the time had come to sell. Wall Street feared the new regulatory body, but Kennedy proved that he could enforce regulation while encouraging business.

The New Dealers rounded out the new financial regulations with the Investment Company Act of 1940 and the Investment Advisers Act of 1940. The latter law extended regulation to mutual funds, which were created in the 1920s but unregulated until this act, and to financial advisors, who were now required to publicly disclose information about investments. The New Deal legislation significantly changed the financial industry and would remain in place for decades.

End of the Gold Standard

One of the scholarly and political debates that still rages is what ended the Great Depression. The New Deal, although successful in addressing some problems and creating some economic growth, did not end the Great Depression. A consensus has emerged that leaving the gold standard helped bring the Depression to an end. Scholars have noted that economic recovery can be dated to a nation leaving the gold standard, with a prime example being Great Britain, which did so in 1931. How is it that throughout the 1920s bankers and diplomats worked diligently to restore the gold standard only to have it unravel during the Depression and later be blamed for the Depression?

The answer lies in the flexibility of the currency. The gold standard had two key virtues that made it "sound money": it tended to be stable and noninflationary. The other argument is that the gold standard made it difficult for politicians to manipulate currencies. While Roosevelt was not an economist, he did understand the need to inflate the currency in the wake of the deflationary stock market crash. To that end, Roosevelt engaged in currency manipulation. Many viewed leaving behind the gold standard as a radical act.

When Roosevelt announced the move to his economics brain trust, they protested loudly and several resigned. The gold standard had been the symbol of sound money for decades.

Roosevelt began, on April 5, by effectively ending the private ownership of gold. He issued an order that private citizens turn in gold coins and gold certificates worth more than $100 to the Federal Reserve for $20.67 per ounce. The government took in $300 million in gold coin and $470 million in certificates, giving the Federal Reserve System a substantial stockpile of gold. In June Congress abrogated the gold clauses in private and public obligations. In 1934 Roosevelt increased the price of gold to $35 per ounce, effectively inflating the money supply. Roosevelt's controversial actions flew in the face of decades of economic orthodoxy, but others agreed that the gold standard needed to go.

The Emergence of Keynes

John Maynard Keynes applauded Roosevelt's actions. For some time, Keynes had been advocating ending the gold standard, earning him a reputation of something of a crackpot among conservative politicians, economists, and bankers. However, Keynes became the economist of the hour during the 1930s. His theories proved so influential and controversial that some credit him with the creation of the modern field of macroeconomics. To this date, economists tend to be categorized by their position on Keynes's ideas.

Keynes began his career in the British civil service in India. From there he became a lecturer at Cambridge. During World War I he worked for the British Treasury. He served as Britain's primary representative on economic matters during the negations over the Treaty of Versailles. Keynes's book, *The Economic Consequences of the Peace,* about the Treaty of Versailles made him a celebrity for his wicked portrayals of the negotiators and dire predictions about the ultimate problems with the reparations system. Keynes began the 1920s as a conventional monetarist, but he became concerned with consistently high unemployment in postwar England. This led Keynes to rethink his position on monetary policy and eventually reject the gold standard in favor of a more flexible currency. Keynes outlined his new thinking in his revolutionary book, *The General Theory of Employment, Interest, and Money.* In this book, Keynes argued that aggregate demand is the function of consumption, investment, and government spending. Therefore, cutting workers' wages reduced consumption, thus weakening the economy. Full employment could be achieved with government spending on public works. Controversially, Keynes argued that governmental deficit spending during economic downturns would fill the shortfall in consumption and investment.

Despite the tendency to associate Keynesian economics with the New Deal, Roosevelt never embraced Keynes. Keynes and Roosevelt met once, leading Keynes to exclaim that Roosevelt did not understand economics and Roosevelt to exclaim that Keynes did not understand politics. Roosevelt viewed deficit spending as an unwelcome necessity during a national emergency.

How Did the New Deal Work?

Explaining the New Deal can be difficult, because Roosevelt experimented so much during his first term. In some ways, it helps to separate the psychology of Roosevelt's leadership from the nuts and bolts of New Deal policy. As we saw with his acceptance speech, Roosevelt did not always propose radically new initiatives, but he addressed the psychology of the Depression with a dramatically more optimistic tone. To this day, the New Deal is vigorously debated. In reality, the New Deal is a mass of policies, some of which contradict each other, done in haste. There are, in fact, stages to the New Deal. Much of the First New Deal emerged from Roosevelt's first hundred days.

Another obstacle for modern readers to understanding the New Deal is the lack of context. Here are several things to keep in mind when considering the New Deal. It is important to remember the desperation people felt, and those desperate people sometimes embraced radical ideas. We tend to associate the rise of radical political extremes, particularly fascism, with Europe. However, throughout the Depression radical political movements in the United States found followers and some calls for a more authoritarian approach to solving the nation's problems. *Gabriel Over the White House,* a popular film in 1933, told the story of a president imposing martial law and creating a fascist state to solve the nation's problems. More than a few people thought the democratic system stood in the way of fixing the economy. The federal government was not a large or vigorous institution. The national government tended to be small and after a decade of Republican emphasis on small government, the federal government lacked what the New Dealers called "state capacity." This is one of the reasons why the New Dealers tended to rely on state and local governments or the military to provide bureaucracy. There existed no easy solution to the Depression, which by Roosevelt's election had entered its fourth year. Some looked to planned economies, such as the communist state in the Soviet Union, while others looked to fascism. Under fascist corporatism society would be organized into corporations, or logical organic units, such as businesses, unions, and so on. These private units would cooperate with each other under the guidance of the government through contracts often obtained through the political party.

Alphabet Soup: First New Deal

Roosevelt's first hundred days launched what historians now refer to as the First New Deal. In his first inaugural, Roosevelt reassured the public that they had nothing to fear but fear itself. He promised bold, persistent experimentation. If something failed he would admit it and move on. Again comparing fighting the Depression with fighting a war, Roosevelt called for action. Roosevelt and the Democrat-controlled congress passed a record amount of legislation during Roosevelt's first hundred days.

The National Industrial Recovery Act, which created the National Recovery Administration held the central position in the New Deal recovery plan. The NIRA tackled several problems that the New Deal brain trust saw as central to the Depression. The act suspended antimonopoly laws, because New Dealers wanted to increase wages and profits. To do so, they needed to curtail competition. The deflationary cycle forced companies into destructive competition that drove down wages and profits. This competition had undermined Hoover's voluntary agreements. In a climate of falling prices and wages, companies found it difficult not to cut wages or prices despite whatever promise they gave the president. Roosevelt sought to end this cycle with the NRA.

The NRA pursued a corporatist solution to the Depression, meaning that the NRA, as a government agency, would organize businesses and unions into groups that agreed to "codes of fair competition" in exchange for exemption to antitrust laws. The NRA was modeled by Congress on the War Industries Board from World War I and had its roots in the Progressive Era belief that excessive competition could be bad. During World War I, the Wilson administration created the board, headed by financier Bernard Baruch, to coordinate economic mobilization. When the war broke out, confusion hindered economic mobilization, so the government stepped in to bring about order, which included nationalizing the railroads. Although the NRA did not nationalize any industry, it did attempt to get business and labor to cooperate as a way of raising profits and wages. Roosevelt appointed retired Army general

The National Recovery Administration was an attempt to change the economy, both in structure and by reversing the psychology of the Depression. The NRA rolled out with much fanfare to encourage people to believe that happy days were here again. *Source:* Unknown, US National Archives and Records Administration, via Wikimedia Commons (public domain).

Hugh Samuel Johnson to direct the NRA. The NRA would oversee public hearings in which companies and labor in a business would create codes of fair competition that covered wages, prices, and hours worked. Part of what made the NIRA controversial is that section 7a recognized the rights of labor unions to participate in the process and engage in collective bargaining. Companies that cooperated with the NRA displayed the blue eagle, a symbol of the NRA, with the slogan "We Do Our Part." Companies failing to display the eagle might be boycotted. The NRA had support from large businesses, which favored cartels because of the elimination of competition and the guarantee of profits. The NRA organized the economy into government-sanctioned cartels to establish price and wage floors.

During the summer of 1933 the NRA started in grand fashion, with parades as Roosevelt announced the President's Preemployment Agreement. Over 2 million employers signed this initial "blanket" code. The codes had a minimum wage of $12 to $15 per week with "share the work" provisions that limited the work week to forty hours. Over its life, the NRA oversaw over 500 codes covering about three-fourths of the nonagricultural economy.

The second part of the NIRA established the Public Works Administration, under the direction of Secretary of the Interior Harold Ickes. The PWA spent about $6 billion on public works such as dams, roads, and other infrastructure. The Emergency Relief Administration, which had been known as the Federal Emergency Relief Administration (FERA) under President Hoover, was given a new name and a new director, Harry Hopkins. Hopkins, from May 1933 to December 1935, awarded grants to states to be used to hire the unskilled and professionals alike. It also provided education for workers. The New Dealers created relief through employment rather than the dole in the belief that the dole would sap a person's will to work. FERA ended in 1935 to be replaced by the Works Progress Administration.

The Civilian Conservation Corps (CCC) was Franklin Roosevelt's favorite New Deal program. The CCC hired young, unmarried men between the ages of eighteen and twenty-five to do environmental work. The US Army oversaw the operation of the CCC; the men lived in camps and barracks. At its peak, the CCC hired 300,000 men, and over 2.5 million men participated during its span from 1933 to 1942. The CCC not only provided employment to young men but also did environmental work such as planting over 3 billion trees and constructing and improving parks.

The Supreme Court struck down the NIRA in *Schechter Poultry Corporation v. the United States* (1935), sometimes referred to as the "sick chicken" case. In its unanimous decision, the court ruled that the NIRA violated the separation of powers in the Constitution. Congress overstepped its bounds in delegating so much authority to the executive branch.

The Agricultural Adjustment Act of 1933 was one of the more controversial New Deal programs. Like the NIRA, the intention of the act was to stabilize and raise prices in order to aid farmers. Farming had been stuck in a deflationary cycle to the point where farmers could not afford to harvest their crops. They would literally lose money in the process. Under the AAA the federal government paid farmers to reduce production, to let fields lie fallow. Farmers had already planted their crops when the legislation passed, meaning that in order to collect the subsidy many plowed under crops and slaughtered farm animals. This did not sit well with urban Americans who were going hungry. The Supreme Court struck down the AAA in *United States v. Butler* on the grounds that a tax on processors used to pay farmer subsidies violated the Tenth Amendment.

Second New Deal

After the Supreme Court invalidated the two major pieces of the New Deal, the NIRA and AAA, in 1935 Roosevelt launched a second round of reform legislation. Some historians argue that the Supreme Court indirectly did Roosevelt a favor in ridding him of a failing NRA, but at the time Roosevelt did not see it that way. The Second New Deal, as it has been called, dealt less with finance and banking but included some of the better-known New Deal legislation. With the Second New Deal, Roosevelt positioned himself for reelection in 1936. The National Labor Relations Act (aka the Wagner Act) replaced section 7a of the NIRA, establishing the National Labor Relations Board and guaranteeing labor unions the right of collective bargaining. Additionally, but not exclusively, Roosevelt signed the Rural Electrification Act and the Revenue Act of 1935, which increased taxes on the wealthy. Perhaps the best-known act, and the cornerstone of the New Deal's legacy, was the Social Security Act.

The Fall of the House of Morgan

The world of finance had changed dramatically. During the 1920s Wall Street had enjoyed a close relationship with the national government. No institution better exemplified this than J. P. Morgan and Company. In many ways, J. P. Morgan partners had acted as extensions of the State Department, especially during times of crisis. The company played an important role in the attempts to settle the German reparations, the Dawes Plan and the Young Plan. Morgan partners had grown accustomed to having access to high-ranking government officials, not just in the United States but also throughout Europe. This ended with the Roosevelt administration. To the extent that the administration associated with Wall Street, it was with Wall Street outsiders such as Joseph Kennedy and Secretary of the Treasury Henry Morgenthau. With both Kennedy and Morgenthau, their ethnic and religious backgrounds contributed to their outsider status. Ethnic and religious tensions lurked just below the surface throughout the political turmoil.

The New Deal struck at several important business practices that J. P. Morgan and Company valued. The first of these was privacy. Morgan partners, and customers, preferred to operate in private. The new laws forced them out into the light, in effect devaluing Morgan's cachet as a banker businessmen could trust. It also eliminated such things as preferred lists, a major perk of being a Morgan client. The mandate separating commercial banking from investment banking damaged J. P. Morgan and Company. The company's chief benefit to its exclusive and private clientele had been its ability to provide full service, to act as both a commercial bank and an investment bank. J. P. Morgan, now in his late sixties and semiretired, and Thomas Lamont, the senior partner, put off making a decision for as long as possible but finally, they decided that J. P. Morgan and Company would be a commercial bank. A separate company, Morgan Stanley, would be created to serve as an investment bank.

It appears that the Morgan partners chose this course of action, which did not bode well for J. P. Morgan and Company, out of the belief that at some point the Glass-Steagall Act would go away, perhaps with the election of a friendlier Republican administration, and that this arrangement would make merging the two easiest. This, however, isn't clear. What is clear is that J. P. Morgan operated in an anemic world of commercial banking on Wall Street while Morgan Stanley benefited from the Morgan name and capital as an investment bank.

Franklin D. Roosevelt won a landslide victory in 1936, pushing further into the future any hopes the bankers had for a friendlier administration. On October 1, 1936, on the eve of the election, Roosevelt, in a major speech announcing the Second New Deal, said:

> We had to struggle with the old enemies of peace—business and financial monopoly, speculation, reckless banking, class antagonism, sectionalism, war profiteering.
>
> They had begun to consider the Government of the United States as a mere appendage to their own affairs. We know now that Government by organized money is just as dangerous as Government by organized mob.
>
> Never before in all our history have these forces been so united against one candidate as they stand today. They are unanimous in their hate for me—and I welcome their hatred.
>
> I should like to have it said of my first Administration that in it the forces of

selfishness and of lust for power met their match. I should like to have it said of my second Administration that in it these forces met their master.

How Do We Explain the New Deal?

As mentioned previously, Franklin Roosevelt became president as the economy bottomed out. The economy grew during these years. Although unemployment remained stubbornly high, the Gross National Product (GNP) by 1937 had exceeded its 1929 level. It appeared that, although problems remained with the economy, things were headed in the right direction. Although there is a tendency to associate Roosevelt's New Deal with Keynesian economics, Roosevelt never fully embraced it. Roosevelt completely abandoned a faith in balanced budgets, so in 1937 he began cutting back on New Deal relief spending, and 1938 saw the Roosevelt Recession. However, by 1939 military spending in Europe increased as World War II spurred on economic growth.

One of the ironies is that Franklin Roosevelt, like Herbert Hoover, failed to end the Great Depression. People often ask, "Did the New Deal work?" In some ways that is the wrong question. The New Deal did not end the Great Depression, but it did bring many changes to the United States. Roosevelt set out three goals for the New Deal: reform, relief, and recovery. Politically, the New Deal proved extraordinarily successful for the Democratic Party. Roosevelt's New Deal coalition dominated the political landscape for a decade. The New Deal also brought about the broker state, with the national government acting as an arbiter between powerful economic groups. Labor unions benefited enormously from the Wagner Act. New Deal programs, beyond a doubt, provided relief for the unemployed. Critics argue that relief artificially inflated wages, thus keeping people unemployed, but for many, working on the Civilian Conservation Corps or similar agencies provided needed wages. Social Security helped transform old age. The banking reforms transformed banking. Although unpopular with bankers—they would lobby for decades to see the Glass-Steagall Act repealed in 1999—the United States went through a long period without financial panics.

Tragically, the Great Depression came to an end only with the Second World War. Massive wartime expenditures combined with the drafting of many men out of the workforce ended the problem of unemployment.

Epilogue: How This Time Is (Not) Different

History Repeats

IN SEPTEMBER 2008, in a scene weighted with historical irony and drama, secretary of the treasury and former president and CEO of Goldman Sachs, Hank Paulson, knelt before Speaker of the House Nancy Pelosi, begging her to support a congressional bailout of Wall Street. Not for the first time, the financial sector faced collapse. To stop the panic, Paulson needed money to shore up the markets. Paulson's begging showed less dignity than Richard Whitney's walk onto the trading floor in October 1929 to buy US Steel, but the underlying issues were the same. Speculation had gotten out of control. The bursting bubble threatened the entire economy, so Paulson wanted an infusion of cash to end the panic. The bailout reflected the debate over the marriage of Wall Street and Washington, which is as old as the republic. The financial sector's collapse brought to the fore the political and economic debates from the Great Depression; the lessons of October 1929 seemed less abstract in the months following September 2008.

Paulson served in the waning days of George W. Bush's presidency. Bush, like his 1920s Republican predecessors, often turned to bankers and business-men to staff his administration. Paulson fit this model, being named secretary of the treasury because of his background at Goldman Sachs. In policies that Harding, Coolidge, and Hoover would have approved, Bush sought to use gov-ernment in support of business and use the stock market to have the wealth it generated become a general prosperity. In his first term, Bush signed the American Dream Downpayment Act, which would, as he said, make it easier for low-income Americans to get home loans; because homeownership "is good for America, it is good for our families, it is good for our economy."[1] Fol-lowing his reelection, President Bush proposed initiatives that would have expanded the investor democracy (he didn't call it that) by allowing people to invest their Social Security savings in the financial sector, where it could see larger returns. Social Security, the trademark New Deal program, continued to be so popular that politicians feared changing it, journalists calling it the "third rail" of American politics. Putting that money in the markets would have marked a major shift in social policy, one that Congress rejected.

In 2008 the failure to invest the Social Security fund in the stock market seemed a good thing. People tuning into the news would have learned that, as the housing bubble burst, financial institutions' proprietary investments in mortgage-backed derivatives quickly transformed into troubled assets. The highly leveraged investment firms had hedged their risks with credit default swaps. In plain English, the giant "banks" bet big, often with borrowed or depositors' money, on investments based on mortgages under the assumption that mortgages are safe investments. Not only were mortgages a historically safe bet, but investors assumed that housing prices would only continue to rise. Both assumptions were too good to be true. Mortgages had been deregu-lated, and banks were giving out mortgages like candy, so the investments built on them were not trustworthy. Eventually, people could not borrow any more money to finance increasingly expensive homes. Just in case, the banks had purchased insurance called credit default swaps, but as it turned out, the insurance companies lacked the resources to honor the deal, so they also went broke. In fact, the distinction between a bank and an insurance com-pany (or even a car company such as GM) had become almost meaningless. A lot of really big companies had decided that easy profits could be found in manipulating money but in doing so had lined themselves up as financial dominoes all in a row. Hank Paulson needed to stop the dominoes from top-pling. Putting aside the specific actors and looking at the actions, this should have been familiar to a student of the 1929 crash. Speculators found new ways to leverage debt to make easy money, building a financial house of cards. Just as we saw with the administrations of Coolidge and Hoover, in retrospect people asked why the government officials did not step in to stop what was obviously going to be a trainwreck.

As the financial sector collapsed internationally, the Bush administration went to Congress seeking a bailout for the massive financial firms that had been deemed "too big to fail." The first votes on the bailout revealed a split among conservatives. In an election year, the president's own party balked at a bailout. House Republicans, disciples of free markets and personal responsibility and heirs to a populist distrust of Wall Street, refused to let the banks off the hook at the taxpayers' expense. Following Paulson's request and with the fate of the nation's economy at stake, Pelosi rallied her Democratic supporters to pass the highly unpopular bailout. As in 1929, the politicians asked what the role of the government in financial markets should be. Where is the line between private gain and risk and public good? Debating these questions often becomes more about politics and ideology than about understanding history. Some scholars argue that "the political rules determine the economic rules." A politician's or policy maker's ideology is often rigid, evidence rarely leads to an altered worldview, while a changing world can lead to market corrections. Thus, ideologues search in the past to support their positon not to find solutions. They are often transformed from political enablers to obstacles to reform.[2]

The Wealth of Nations and the Delusions of Crowds

When Congress took up the bailout of Wall Street, it revisited an age-old debate among bankers and politicians negotiating the relationship between finance and politics. Does the financial sector serve the nation? What responsibility do bankers have to the common good? Who pays the bill for a crashed bubble? By the time Adam Smith wrote *An Inquiry into the Nature and Causes of the Wealth of Nations* (1776), Europe had already seen multiple bubbles burst. Charles Mackay's *Extraordinary Popular Delusions and the Madness of Crowds (1841)* pointed to these earlier speculative bubbles. As we've already seen, Mackay's book was a favorite among speculators. Mackay looked at the Dutch tulip mania in the 1600s and speculation in New World markets and money. In Holland otherwise rational people bet huge sums on the color of flower a tulip bulb would produce. Later, we saw speculative manias grip the

French and the English. The speculative frenzies were explained, according to Mackay, by the same popular delusions and madness that accounted for witch hunts, alchemy, and fortune telling.

In the twenty-first century, Mackay still has his followers, who see the mania of the crowd as the fundamental explanation for speculation. The motivation for the twenty-first century housing bubble is more or less the same as for the seventeenth-century tulip bubble. Unlike the other subjects of his book, witch hunting and alchemy, which both declined with modernity, speculative frenzies have not gone away but have gotten larger and more frequent. Crowds in Europe or America rarely develop a mania for witch trials anymore, but they continue to engage in speculation.

The appeal of Mackay is that he offers a timeless explanation grounded in human nature. It is a simple explanation for events that often seem wildly convoluted. You don't need to understand credit default swaps to understand that people go nuts when they think they can make a lot of easy money. He isn't alone in looking for an explanation. Over the years we've developed metaphors to explain a speculative crisis. Much in the same way that Adam Smith discussed markets as forces of nature, something beyond human control or certainly something it is not wise to meddle with, the metaphors evoke catastrophic weather (the perfect storm), a disease (a contagion), or a nuclear catastrophe (a meltdown). It seems that we cannot find a metaphor big enough for the problem, which is surprising because we have been discussing the globalization of markets for at least a generation. For years we have been celebrating the efficient flow of money through global markets, not seeming to realize that the contagion of a crash could spread through them just as easily as investment capital. Similar to 1929, the 2008 contagion spread to become a "global financial meltdown."

Mackay reminds us of the importance of remembering previous bubbles. As we have seen, forgetting the last panic is a precondition of the new bubble. When considering the history of speculation, another cliché, that hindsight is 20/20, seems appropriate. However, the clarity that exists shortly after a speculative bubble bursts rarely lasts. As we move from the event, hindsight becomes fuzzy, and disagreement emerges over the causes. Perhaps the disagreement contributes to the collective amnesia that afflicts society the next time speculation starts and money flows. When a person stands up to say, "The last time this happened, it did not end well," he or she will be dismissed, if not ridiculed. For the sake of not forgetting, let's dissect the 2008 financial crisis using the lesson of 1929 and other meltdowns.

The 1920s and 1930s are fascinating, not only because of the boom followed by the bust, but also because of the dichotomy of the politics of a conservative, probusiness era followed by the progressive New Deal era. While many scholars point to ways in which the two bleed together, for example, Hoover's policies foreshadowing the New Deal, the binary nature of our two-party system lends itself to an either/or debate: free markets or regulation, Friedrich Hayek or John Maynard Keynes, minimalist government or activist government. The need to vote for one or the other encourages us to impose this vision on the past. We begin our story with the political enablers who looked past the activism of the New Deal to the Republican rule of the 1920s in search of a free-market solution to society's ills.

Political Enablers

After his election in 1980 President Ronald Reagan hung a portrait of Calvin Coolidge in the White House to symbolize the end of the New Deal and the return of trickle-down economics, now dubbed supply-side economics. Reagan admired the small-government policies of the 1920s, and so honored Coolidge over the disgraced Harding and Hoover (disgraced for different reasons). As we saw in the last chapter, the New Deal changed banking significantly, mostly in the direction of reducing risk and profit by increasing regulation. Reagan ushered in a generation of deregulation and free-market policies designed to promote economic growth. National leaders sang the virtues of private enterprise while proclaiming, to paraphrase Reagan, that government was the problem, not the solution. Reaganomics produced mixed results. After a harsh recession in the early 1980s, the economy grew at a significant clip throughout the decade. Thanks to a combination of tax cuts and increased military spending, the federal deficit climbed to new heights. In 1988 Americans elected George H. W. Bush president to carry on Reagan's policies. However, his administration saw the Savings and Loan Crisis rock the financial world; it grew out of a combination of changed tax policies and deregulation. Rallying his supporters with the slogan "It's the economy, stupid," Bill Clinton emerged as a centrist Democrat and defeated Bush, as Americans blamed him for their economic woes.

The Clinton administration oversaw another period of prosperity, called the New Economy, which was dominated by new technologies, this time the Internet. Clinton, however, had imbibed some of the tenets of neoliberal capitalism. He embraced free trade, globalization, and deregulation, declaring that the age of big government was over in his 1996 State of the Union address. He proudly signed the North American Free Trade Agreement (NAFTA). He also balanced the budget and produced a budget surplus.

In 1999 President Clinton signed the Gramm-Leach-Bliley Act it, which overturned the Glass-Steagall Act, one of the signature New Deal pieces of legislation meant to curb the excesses of speculation by bankers. The Glass-Steagall Act had separated investment banks from commercial banks so that commercial banks could not speculate with other people's money; it was one of the remaining vestiges of the government's response to the 1929 crash. In the long term, the Gramm-Leach-Bliley Act set the stage for banks evolving into gigantic financial institutions that were dubbed "too big to fail." Proponents of repealing the Glass-Steagall Act argued that in a global economy, it hindered the ability of American banks to modernize and compete. The dot. com bubble bursting in 2000 overshadowed changes to the banking industry, but the changes had long-term importance. The emergence of the commercial viability of the Internet changed the rules of the economic game, leading to more speculation. Many dot.com startups eventually failed. Clinton, however, left office in 2000. His successor, George W. Bush, continued to pursue deregulation.

The Housing Bubble

Both political parties pursued policies that contributed to the housing bubble. Why? Historically, Americans have placed a great deal of value on property ownership; from the yeoman farmer to the suburban developer, Americans believed in property as the key to an independent and prosperous citizenry. The American middle class built its wealth in its homes. No politician opposed something as American as homeownership. Therefore, when housing prices rose political leaders celebrated, rather than warning that a housing bubble might be underway. In desirable parts of the country, housing prices climbed dramatically, seemingly producing an endless source of wealth for middle-class Americans. The feeling of never-ending wealth and easy access to home equity loans based on inflated prices drove the market upward and fueled consumption. Want a new pool? Buy it with a home equity loan. Pay for that dream vacation with a home equity loan. Several factors drove the housing bubble. Tax laws favored homeownership and use of home equity loans, which were made more attractive by the prospects of ever-increasing values. Mortgage interest rates were at historic lows. Deregulation of the financial industry helped increase access to easy money in the form of the spread of subprime mortgages for borrowers who could not have afforded a mortgage under the old rules.

After 2008 the debates emerged: did a policy failure or a market failure cause the bubble and crash? In part this debate misses the point that the private and public sectors collaborated to create the crisis. The crash denoted a failure of policy and a failure of markets.

Mortgages were no longer the purview of local savings and loans and local bankers; both had been replaced by enormous multinational financial institutions. Now mortgage brokers worked to find potential homeowners loans. Sales teams looked to put customers in a mortgage. Real estate brokers guaranteed that the prices would only go higher; one needed to buy sooner rather than later. Once the bank secured the mortgage, the bank bundled it and sold it on international markets. A mortgage loan originating in Indiana might find its way to London. Since banks no longer held the mortgages, their incentives became commissions and not the interest made by holding the mortgage for decades. Banks no longer needed to guarantee that the person who borrowed the money could repay the money. Whoever invested in the bundled mortgages, or the derivatives from the mortgages, assumed the risk, often without understanding it. With this incentive, financial professionals and real estate agents found it advantageous to get people into houses regardless of their down payment, income, or much of anything else. With most of the public not noticing it, the home mortgage had gone from one of the safest, most conservative investments to a high-risk financial instrument. Rating agencies, such as Standard & Poor's, continued to give mortgages their top ratings.

Sweat Equity

Policy makers and bankers saw political and financial reasons to put people in homes, but others boosted the housing boom as well. Boosterism had not gone away. The "this time is different" attitude helped people ignore the problems compounding in the housing and financial markets. If Sinclair Lewis wrote in the twenty-first century, Babbitt might have had a TV show. The Internet made the booster's medium of choice, the local newspaper, obsolete.

The medium had changed, but the message echoed from the 1920s. Celebrity investors found a home on cable television, hocking stocks and touting the virtues of the can't-fail market. One has to wonder what the staid Morgan partners, who disdained advertising and worked at rolltop desks, where they did not remove their jackets, would have thought of *Mad Money*, featuring Jim Cramer, jacketless and with his sleeves rolled up, yelling buy or sell while punching props to create sound effects. Is *Mad Money* the madness of the crowd, Mackay's mania? One is reminded of the story about Joseph Kennedy, that he knew it was time to get out of the stock market when he got tips from the shoeshine boy. What would he have thought of call-in talk shows on investing? Although louder and faster, these champions of stocks are the still-recognizable ancestors of the pioneers of the financial reporting in the 1920s, who mixed promoting with reporting.

For those less interested in stocks, television hosts instructed speculators on how to flip a home. These shows combined the conservative, time-honored, middle-class route to financial security of homeownership and sweat equity with the fervor of speculation. *Flip That House* showed people buying and repairing homes to flip, that is to turn them over rapidly for a profit. In the show's narrative, flipping a house carried risk but also the possibility of a handsome reward. The Learning Channel's show *Trading Spaces* did not have open speculation. Contestants would volunteer to redecorate each other's homes with the aid of professional decorators. The show's popularity led to a cross-promotional tie-in with the home improvement megastore chain Home Depot. People were told they should not just live in homes; homes were for investing and not long-term community building.

Since Herbert Hoover

George W. Bush did not pursue more deregulation, but rather seemed content to continue the deregulation of the previous decades. In fact, he signed the Sarbanes-Oxley Act, which tightened regulation of corporate financial reporting in response to the Enron scandal and the subsequent collapse of that company and the accounting firm Arthur Andersen. However, the Bush administration gained a reputation for lax enforcement of regulations. Under George Bush's administration, bankers had an enormous amount of influence over the oversight agencies, continuing a trend from previous administrations. Bankers from the 1920s would have understood the revolving door between the Wall Street firms, the Federal Reserve Board, and the Treasury Department.

George W. Bush advocated creating an "ownership society." Here is another echo of the 1920s. The ownership society had many of the same elements as the investor's democracy ideology that emerged in that decade. If people had an ownership stake, they would take care to be responsible and build their wealth—not quite John J. Raskob's "Everybody Ought to Be Rich" but in a similar spirit. This included investing in the stock market and homeownership, something encouraged by Freddie Mac and Fannie Mae, two giant loan corporations backed by the federal government. There is some irony that at the point in time that Americans celebrated free markets, investment, and property ownership—hallmarks of the investor's democracy—that they also accumulated large debts in both the public and the private sectors.

For decades mortgages had been a conservative investment offering modest returns with little risk. Savings and Loans had carefully loaned money to people who had saved down payments and established credit histories. This world had disappeared over time. Believing that housing prices would climb indefinitely, increasing numbers of Americans bought homes with a growing number of subprime mortgages being issued. No longer did Americans need to put down 20 percent and demonstrate that they were responsibly and gainfully employed. Banks no longer held the mortgages they sold, but instead bundled them into complex financial packages—derivatives—that were sold to investors who falsely believed that the underlying mortgages were sound. In some instances, pension funds and retirement account executors purchased these instruments, believing them to be conservative, secure investments. Other times large financial institutions bet on the derivatives from subprime mortgages simultaneously hedging their bets by taking out insurance in case the investments failed. Again, the investments seemed foolproof. As AIG (American International Group) learned when it provided this insurance through derivative swaps that provided the hedge, these investments were not based on AAA secure mortgages grounded by middle-class Americans saving for and buying homes.

Over a number of years Wall Street speculators had built a highly complex and profitable house of cards. All the while, the familiar refrain of "this time is different" could be heard. Several things made this time "different." Wall Street firms had hired "quants," mathematical wizards, many with scientific backgrounds, who built elaborate mathematical models to predict markets and guide investments. Quants and their models became the new normal on Wall Street. No longer would J. P. Morgan direct the flow of money from the Corner at 23 Wall Street. The titans of finance consulted mathematical oracles, which, in retrospect, it is clear they did not always understand. However, as long as the models seemed foolproof that was okay.

When home prices began to fall and home values went underwater— "underwater" is when a debt owed on a house becomes greater than the market value of the house—the subprime mortgages were exposed as poor investments and the derivatives could, and did, fail. The bursting housing bubble sent ripples through giant banks and insurance companies that threatened the entire financial system. Financial companies that had recently been hailed as "too big to fail" were failing. Panic gripped the financial markets. Computer models failed. Banks had bet on highly complex financial instruments, derivatives based on subprime mortgages, but had hedged their bets with derivative swaps. AIG had sold banks insurance just in case the fail-safe investment failed, and now it had nowhere close to the money needed to pay the claims.

The financial panic underscored the close relationship between Wall Street and Washington. When the bubble crashed in 2008, Hank Paulson was secretary of the treasury. Paulson was the former chief executive of Goldman Sachs. Paulson worked closely with Tim Geithner, director of the New York Federal Reserve Bank, to manage the crisis and implement the bailout package that Congress passed. Geithner had been part of President Clinton's team that oversaw a small international financial crisis. He would go on to be President Barack Obama's secretary of the treasury. Alan Greenspan, the long-standing chairman of the Federal Reserve Board, who had a reputation for masterfully guiding the economy and for his free-market ideology, had stepped down to be replaced by Ben Bernanke. Greenspan's reputation was greatly damaged by the financial panic. Perhaps fortuitously, Bernanke was an academic economist who had studied the Great Depression.

On the insistence of these men, Congress reluctantly passed the Troubled Asset Relief Program, or TARP, to bailout the nation's banks. Under Bernanke the Federal Reserve took the most aggressive steps in its history to bail out and save the financial sector. Paulson and Bernanke did not reluctantly ease their way into fighting the oncoming Depression, as Hoover and the Federal Reserve had in the early 1930s. They flooded the street with money, believing that similar methods had worked in the crisis of the 1980s and 1990s. It became clear that Wall Street understood that the risks and debts it took while speculating were, de facto, covered by the US government. However, the Federal Reserve made a mistake in allowing Lehman Brothers to go under. Paulson and Bernanke were concerned that bankers would not learn the lessons of their reckless behavior by paying the price for it; in economics this is referred to as "moral hazard." Therefore, they decided not to bail out Lehman Brothers. When the bankers learned that the government might not cover their losses, the result was a tremendous loss of confidence, leading to the government bailout of AIG, which had insured the financial firms' losses. For the nation, this meant a freezing of credit and a disaster for companies that depended on people borrowing money. The American automobile industry approached collapse, which led to a bailout of General Motors and Chrysler.

In his final White House press conference, President Bush asked, "Why did the financial collapse have to happen on my watch?" According to one reporter in *Time* magazine, "George Bush is leaving the White House with a dismal economic record. By almost every measure—GDP growth, jobs, median incomes, financial-market performance—he stacks up as probably the least-successful President on the economic front since Herbert Hoover."[3]

Politics of Anger

Herbert Hoover promised the American people prosperity just before the prosperity ended. Franklin Roosevelt assured Americans that they had nothing to fear. In the wake of the 9/11 tragedy, George W. Bush told Americans to go shopping. More than a few people have noted that hard times bring out the jeremiad, lamenting the state of things often attributed to moral or ethical decline. Hard times bring anger. In many ways each is an individual episode with unique characteristics, but there are areas of overlap that make it possible to discuss the general using a specific case study. During the elections of 2010, Tea Party protestors evoking the American Revolution served as a reminder of the vigor that Americans have long debated the nature of the economy and the role of the government in it. Entering the 2012 political cycle, the Occupy Wall Street movement protested policies that favor the top 1 percent of the US population over the bottom 99 percent. In many ways, the protestors followed in the footsteps of the progressives, with their distrust of the money trust, but also past protest movements fueled by economic hard times such as the People's Party and Coxey's Army after the Panic of 1893.

Globalized Crisis

In echoes of the late 1920s, some of the earlier warnings regarding a speculative bubble took place in Europe. In March 2007 European banks, including HSBC (Hongkong and Shanghai Banking Corporation), warned that instability in the subprime mortgage markets in the United States was hindering their ability to meet their target earnings. London and Wall Street have long been connected, but in the twenty-first century transatlantic banking was easier and faster than ever. Bankers could avoid regulations by crossing national boundaries. In a lesson that J. P. Morgan could have taught, European bankers and US policy makers were about to be reminded of how large and international financial markets had become. In 2008 Europeans and Americans experienced the downside of the globalized financial markets.

Herbert Hoover, as previously noted, blamed Europe for the Great Depression. Hoover's observation echoed in the twenty-first century as European banks fell to the crisis. Technological changes to global markets made Icelandic banks relevant to Americans. Iceland had transformed itself from a fishing economy to a hub of international monetary speculation. The same technologies that made the world flat with globalization also made its financial markets deeply interconnected. The contagion spread from the US housing crisis as those derivatives were sold globally. As a result, the Celtic Tiger of Ireland saw its economy go from boom to bust. Bank panics broke out in the Netherlands and Great Britain.

The 2008 financial panic reached across the Atlantic, merging into the ongoing Eurozone debt crisis. When Hoover blamed the Depression on Europe, he was referring to the debt and currency crisis that followed World War I. The Great War and the Treaty of Versailles set up an unviable international financial system in which the British and the French owed American banks more money than they could repay. To repay those loans, the victorious nations imposed heavy reparations on Germany that Germany could not afford to pay. The reparation burden ultimately led to the demise of Germany's economy. As Hoover saw it, the European house of cards crumbled, taking with it the American banking system. For Hoover this explanation has the virtue of explaining that the Great Depression was someone else's fault, but it is relevant to today following the collapse of American finance and the unfolding of the Eurozone crisis. Much like the Greek and Spanish governments today, the British and the French argued that their debt should be restructured. The Americans, much like today's German government or the European Central Bank, insisted on repayment and when that proved impossible reluctantly agreed to deals that eased but did not solve the crisis.

Exit the Maestro, Enter the Master?

Journalist Bob Woodward titled his book on Alan Greenspan *Maestro: Greenspan's Fed and the American Boom* to highlight his role in managing the economy. After 2008 the title became ironic. Greenspan had been part of a generation of economists who had rejected Keynesian-style planning in favor of free markets, or in the case of Greenspan, who favored the philosophy of Ayn Rand, whom he knew and admired earlier in his life. The decades following the Great Depression saw the rise of Keynesian economics and the counterrevolution in classical economics that energized American political debate on the appropriate role of the government in the economy. However, by the 1980s Keynes was completely out of fashion; monetarist economists such as Milton Friedman were now in. This changed after the 2008 crash. As the giants of Wall Street collapsed, treasury and Federal Reserve officials quickly moved to intervene, with seemingly little thought to letting the markets take their course.

Keynes, and to an extent Hayek, when confronted with the Great Depression rethought the field of economics. Franklin Roosevelt, conceding that his programs did not end the Depression, successfully managed the politics of anger and extremism of the 1930s. While some nations turned to fascism, Roosevelt offered the Civilian Conservation Corps and Social Security. What I suggest is that the Panic of 2008 has produced surprisingly little in the way of fresh thinking. Ideological rigidity and caution, rather than bold experimentation, have led few to question the underlying assumptions that helped create the problem in the first place.

Another way to think about this is that, despite the rhetoric to the contrary, Wall Street has always had deep ties to the national government. This goes back to the Washington administration and the policies of Alexander Hamilton. Many a politician has pandered to voters by bashing Wall Street, but as often as not the Wall Street banker has had the ear of the politician. While we may want to apply grand ideas, this could come down to a few simple ideas that can be found in Jesse Livermore's favorite book, Charles

Mackay's *Extraordinary Popular Delusions and the Madness of Crowds.* People will speculate when there is easy money to be had. When these things happen, history will repeat, even as we tell ourselves that this time it is different. When the speculative bubble bursts, people will panic and that panic will spur the crash.

NOTES

PROLOGUE: HOW PANIC SPREADS

1. John Kenneth Galbraith, *The Great Crash, 1929* (Mariner, 2009 [1954]), 130.

CHAPTER ONE. HOW IN THE 1920S THE AMERICAN ECONOMY
PROMOTED SPECULATION

1. Herbert Hoover, *The Memoirs of Herbert Hoover: The Great Depression, 1929–1941* (MacMillan, 1952), 2; available at www.ecommcode.com/hoover/ebooks/pdf/FULL/B1V3 _Full.pdf; see also David M. Kennedy, *Freedom from Fear: The American People in Depression and War, 1929–1945* (Oxford, 1999), 9.

2. Maury Klein, *Rainbow's End: The Crash of 1929* (Oxford, 2001), 25.

3. Beverly Gage, *The Day Wall Street Exploded: A Story of America in Its First Age of Terror* (Oxford, 2009), 1.

4. It is worth noting that Coolidge also cleaned up the administration as several officials from the Harding administration were engulfed by scandals.

CHAPTER TWO. HOW BUSINESS CULTURE ENCOURAGED CONSUMER SPENDING

1. Bureau of Labor Statistics, www.bls.gov/opub/cwc/cm20030124ar03p1.htm.

CHAPTER THREE. HOW THE MARKET GREW BULLISH

1. Julia C. Ott, *When Wall Street Met Main Street: The Quest for an Investor's Democracy* (Cambridge, 2011), 7.

2. Ron Chernow, *House of Morgan: An American Banking Dynasty and the Rise of Modern Finance* (Atlantic Monthly Press, 1990), 24.

3. Maury Klein, *Rainbow's End: The Crash of 1929* (Oxford, 2001), 46.

4. "Meehan, Broker, Ill in Sanitarium," *New York Times,* November 25, 1936, http://query.nytimes.com/mem/archive/pdf?res=F40616FA3C5A1B7B93C7AB178AD95F4283 85F9.

5. "Stutz Settlement Rumors Unverified," *New York Times,* April 6, 1920, http://query.nytimes.com/mem/archive-free/pdf?res=F40911F63A55157A93C4A9178FD85F44 8285F9; "Allan A. Ryan Fails," *New York Times,* July 22, 1922, http://query.nytimes.com /mem/archive-free/pdf?res=F30716FC395D1A7A93C0AB178CD85F468285F9.

6. "Piggly Wiggly Saunders Fought to Bitter End," *New York Times,* August 26, 1923,

http://query.nytimes.com/mem/archive/pdf?res=F50910F73F5416738DDDAF0A94D04
05B838EF1D3.

7. Samuel Crowther, "Everybody Ought to Be Rich: An Interview with John J. Raskob," *Ladies' Home Journal* (August 1929), http://wp.lps.org/kbeacom/files/2012/08/Everybody OughtToBeRich.pdf.

8. Committee on Recent Economic Changes of the President's Conference on Unemployment, *Recent Economic Changes in the United States,* Volumes 1 and 2 (Washington, DC: Government Printing Office, 1929): xii, www.nber.org/books/comm29-1.

9. "Alexander D. Noyes of the Times Dead," *New York Times,* April 23, 1945, http://query.nytimes.com/mem/archive/pdf?res=F50A1FF73C5D177A93C1AB178FD85F4184
85F9.

10. "Clarence W. Barron, Publisher, Is Dead," *New York Times,* October 3, 1928, http://query.nytimes.com/mem/archive/pdf?res=F10C16F6355E14728FDDAA0894D8415B888
EF1D3.

11. Crowther, "Everybody Ought to Be Rich," 236.

12. Crowther, "Everybody Ought to Be Rich," 238.

13. Crowther, "Everybody Ought to Be Rich," 239.

CHAPTER FOUR. HOW THE ECONOMY CRASHED

1. Robert Sobel, *The Big Board: A History of the New York Stock Market* (Beard, 1965), 235.

2. John Kenneth Galbraith, *The Great Crash, 1929* (Mariner, 2009 [1954]), 21.

3. Galbraith, *The Great Crash,* 11.

4. Galbraith, *The Great Crash,* 1.

5. Galbraith, *The Great Crash,* 16.

6. Galbraith, *The Great Crash,* 72.

7. Frederick Lewis Allen, *Only Yesterday: An Informal History of the 1920s* (Blue Ribbon, 1931), http://xroads.virginia.edu/~HYPER/ALLEN/ch13.html.

8. Galbraith, *The Great Crash,* 27.

9. Galbraith, *The Great Crash,* 28.

10. Galbraith, *The Great Crash,* 37.

11. Galbraith, *The Great Crash,* 40.

12. "Garment Union Chief Sees Benefit in Crash," *New York Times,* October 31, 1929, http://query.nytimes.com/mem/archive/pdf?res=F30B17FE3D5F177A93C3AA178BD95F
4D8285F9.

13. "Business Gain Seen by Freeing of Funds," *New York Times,* November 6, 1929, http://query.nytimes.com/mem/archive/pdf?res=FB0B1FFC3454127A93C4A9178AD95F
4D8285F9.

14. Allen, *Only Yesterday.*

CHAPTER FIVE. HOW THE NEW DEAL CHANGED THE FINANCIAL SECTOR

1. "FDR and the Democratic National Convention," In Roosevelt History: Sharing the Franklin D. Roosevelt Presidential Library and Museum Collections and Programs," https://fdrlibrary.files.wordpress.com/2012/09/1932.pdf.

2. "FDR and the Democratic National Convention."

3. Maury Klein, *Rainbow's End: The Crash of 1929* (Oxford, 2001), 215.

4. Hearings, US Senate, Committee on Banking and Currency, Hearings May 23–25, 1933 (Washington, DC: Government Printing Office, 1933): 6. Also available on Google Books at https://books.google.com/books?id=Hc8PAAAAIAAJ.

EPILOGUE. HOW THIS TIME IS (NOT) DIFFERENT

1. George W. Bush, "Remarks on Signing the American Dream Downpayment Act," December 16, 2003, Public Papers of the Presidents of the United States, National Archives and Records Administration, Office of the Federal Register (Washington, DC: Government Printing Office), 1733. It is also available on Google Books.

2. Nolan McCarty, Keith T. Poole, and Howard Rosenthal, *Political Bubbles: Financial Crises and the Failure of American Democracy* (Princeton, 2013), 17.

3. Justin Fox, "A Look Back at Bush's Economic Missteps," *Time,* January 19, 2009, www.time.com/time/specials/packages/article/0,28804,1872229_1872230,00.html.

SUGGESTED FURTHER READING

In the wake of the 2008 crash there emerged an extensive literature on speculation. However, it is worth starting with Charles Mackay's *Memoirs of Extraordinary Popular Delusions and the Madness of Crowds* (1841). Because it has long since passed into the public domain, you have the option of reading it online through web pages such as Project Gutenberg (www.gutenberg.org/ebooks/24518). Although written in the nineteenth century, Mackay's book on mass psychology still offers insight into the human nature behind speculation and panics. Before diving into popular delusions such as alchemy and witchcraft, he looks at early bubbles such as the Mississippi Scheme, the South Sea Bubble, and Tulipomania. Understanding the Dutch tulip craze helps understand more recent crashes, in that many writers referenced Tulipomania when covering the 2008 crash. A more recent treatment of speculation is Carmen M. Reinhart and Kenneth S. Rogoff's *This Time Is Different: Eight Centuries of Financial Folly* (Princeton, 2009). For more on panics, see Robert Sobel's *Panic on Wall Street: A History of America's Financial Disasters* (Beard, 1969 [1999]). Sobel offers insight into financial panics from 1792 to 1962, helping place the 1929 crash in context and reinforcing looking at general trends of how speculation and panics work. In *Wheels of Fortune: The History of Speculation from Scandal to Respectability* (Wiley, 2002), Charles R. Geist looks at various speculators from the nineteenth to the twentieth century. Robert J. Shiller's *Irrational Exuberance* (2nd edition, Doubleday, 2005) is an examination of market volatility. In *Devil Take the Hindmost: A History of Financial Speculation* (Plume, 2000) Edward Chancellor looks at the history of stock market speculation.

For general histories of Wall Street, a good starting place is Charles R. Geist's *Wall Street: A History from Its Beginnings to the Fall of Enron* (Oxford, 2004). Steve Fraser's *Every Man a Speculator: A History of Wall Street in American Life* (Harper Perennial, 2005) is a good source for looking at the place of Wall Street in US history since the founding of the nation. For another overview of Wall Street, read Robert Sobel's *The Big Board: A History of the New York Stock Market* (Beard Books, 1965 [2000]). Ron Chernow's *The House of Morgan: An American Banking Dynasty and the Rise of Modern Finance* (Atlantic Monthly Press, 1990) offers insights into the evolution of American finance through the Morgan family and their business interest. Julie C. Ott made a valuable contribution to our understanding of the relationship between finance and the rest of society in her *When Wall Street Met Main Street: The Quest for an Investor's Democracy* (Harvard, 2011). Beverly Gage's *The Day Wall Street Exploded: The Story of America in Its First Age of Terror* (Oxford, 2009) is a good examination of the context of Wall Street after World War I.

The House of Morgan obviously represents Wall Street insiders. For more on less reputable dealings, see Mitchell Zuckoff's *Ponzi's Scheme: The True Story of a Financial Legend* (Random House, 2005) and John Brooks's *Once in Golconda: A True Drama of Wall Street, 1920–1938* (Wiley, 1969 [1999]).

When looking at the causes of the 1929 crash and the Great Depression, it is important to look at the central banks and bankers. James K. Galbraith's *The Great Crash, 1929* (Mariner, 1954 [2009]) is a classic Keynesian interpretation of the start of the Great Depression. Galbraith emphasizes the delusions that fueled the mania and panic. Liaquat Ahamed's *Lords of Finance: The Bankers Who Broke the World* (Penguin, 2009) looks at the role of central bankers but does a good job laying out the international banking situation as it was stressed following World War I. Maury Klein's *Rainbow's End: The Crash of 1929* (Oxford, 2001) offers a strong narrative of the crash.

When considering changes to the banking system prior to the 1920s, a good place to start is Louis D. Brandeis's *Other People's Money and How the Bankers Use It*, ed. Melvin Urofsky (Bedford, 1985). Brandeis's influence on the policies of Woodrow Wilson and Franklin Roosevelt makes this a valuable read. Brandeis wrote in the wake of the Panic of 1907, which Robert F. Bruner and Sean D. Carr examine in *The Panic of 1907: Lessons Learned from the Market's Perfect Storm* (Wiley, 2007). Although students may find it a daunting read, Allan H. Meltzer's *A History of the Federal Reserve*, vol. 1: *1913–1951* is a treasure trove of information on that institution. Also on the topic of the Federal Reserve is Robert L. Hetzel's *The Monetary Policy of the Federal Reserve: A History* (Cambridge, 2008).

Roland Marchand's *Advertising the American Dream: Making Way for Modernity, 1919–1940* (University of California Press, 1986) is a good examination of the role of advertising in creating postwar expectations in the consumer culture. Frederick Lewis Allen's *Only Yesterday: An Informal History of the Nineteen-Twenties* (Blue Ribbon, 1931) is a classic journalistic account of the 1920s that still remains useful.

David Kennedy's *Freedom from Fear: The American People in Depression and War, 1929–1945* (Oxford, 1999) is an excellent examination of the Great Depression and World War II. Robert S. McElvaine's *The Great Depression: America, 1929–1941* (Times, 1984) is a positive interpretation of the New Deal. A critical view of the New Deal can be found in Amity Shlaes's *The Forgotten Man: A New History of the Great Depression* (HarperCollins, 2007). John A. Garraty, *The Great Depression* (Anchor Books, 1987), offers an overview of the 1930s. Ellis Hawley is a preeminent scholar of the period. His *The New Deal and the Problem of Monopoly* (Princeton, 1966) offers insight into the difficulties confronted by New Deal policy makers. Another classic is Arthur M. Schlesinger's three-volume *The Age of Roosevelt*. Schlesinger is largely favorable toward the New Deal and Roosevelt. His massive work offers a great deal of information.

On John Maynard Keynes and his debate with Friedrich Hayek, see Nicholas Wapshott's *Keynes Hayek: The Clash that Defined Modern Economics* (Norton, 2011). Robert Skidelsky is perhaps the most prominent biographer of Keynes. He has written several books on Keynes, but his *Keynes: The Return of the Master* outlines his views on the relationship of Keynesian economics to the 2008 crisis.

The 2008 crash has produced an enormous amount of writing. It is worth noting that Ben Bernanke, who was head of the Federal Reserve Board during the meltdown is a scholar of the Great Depression; see his *Essays on the Great Depression* (Princeton, 2000). As a starting point, consider Alan S. Blinder's *After the Music Stopped: The Financial Crisis, the Response, and the Work Ahead* (Penguin, 2013) and Andrew Ross Sorkin's *Too Big to Fail: The Inside Story of How Wall Street and Washington Fought to Save the Financial System— and Themselves* (Penguin, 2010). John Cassidy's *How Markets Fail: The Logic of Economic Calamities* (Farrar, Straus and Giroux, 2009) examines the rise of "utopian economics." In looking at the relationship between politicians and finance, consider Nolan McCarty, Keith T. Poole, and Howard Rosenthal's *Political Bubbles: Financial Crisis and the Failure of American Democracy* (Princeton, 2013).

INDEX

Page numbers in *italics* refer to illustrations.